Wings Across *the* Border

An American's Travels to See Mexico's Birds

Stauffer Miller

With Illustrations by Catherine Gausman

WINGS ACROSS THE BORDER:
AN AMERICAN'S TRAVELS TO SEE MEXICO'S BIRDS

Stauffer Miller

with illustrations by Catherine Gausman

To order additional copies of this book, contact:
Xlibris
844-714-8691
www.Xlibris.com
Orders@Xlibris.com

ISBN: Softcover   978-1-6698-1850-2
         Hardcover   978-1-6698-1849-6
         EBook   978-1-6698-1851-9
Library of Congress Control Number: 2022906097
Print information available on the last page

Rev. date: 04/14/2022

Also by Stauffer Miller

Hoisting Their Colors: Cape Cod's Civil War Navy Officers

Cape Cod and the Civil War: The Raised Right Arm

Sandwich Soldiers, Sailors, Sons: A Cape Cod Town in the Civil War

CONTENTS

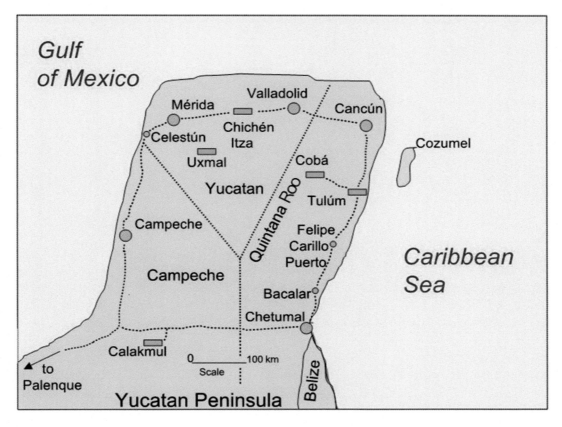

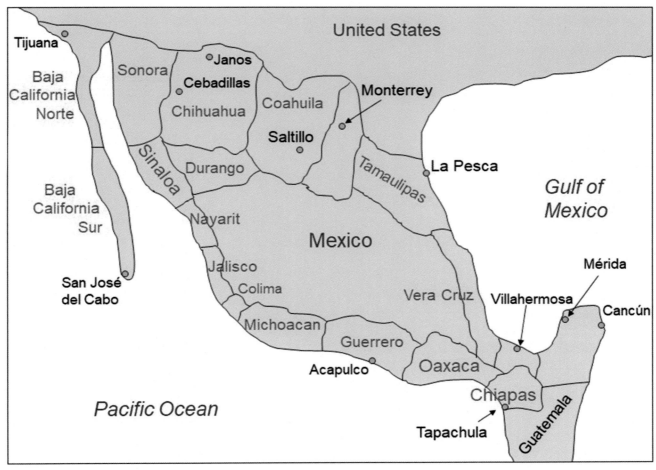

FOREWORD

• ● •

Travel and birding have entwined themselves in my life. Much of my travel has been to see birds, and much of my birding has entailed travel. The two have complemented each other. I even met my wife, Ellie, through travel to Utah. And to do what? You guessed it, to see birds.

After we were married in 1978, the two of us continued to travel, almost always with birds as a focus; and by 1986, we had journeyed to most of the United States and much of Canada and, in so doing, seen many of the bird species in those places. A great chapter in our lives seemed to have closed. So what next? It was while we stood at this juncture that a chance encounter occurred, one that planted the idea of opening a new chapter: travel to see Mexico and its birds. And that long chapter is the subject of this writing.

I am dedicating this book to Ellie. She taught me much about birds and birding. Furthermore, once she heard about Mexico and its bird attractions, she was all in. She loved our adventures there and encouraged me to continue going when she no longer could. And once I got going with the book, her daughter, Connie, helped with all manner of technical assistance.

I would also like to acknowledge the many American bird tour company guides who found and pointed out to me, and us, birds in every corner of Mexico. I have listed those guides in the appendix. While I enjoy immensely finding birds on my own, sometimes you just need professional help, certainly with the more unusual and secretive species. I heartily recommend employing guides. With time, more will be Mexican, as it should be.

Around one thousand bird species have been recorded for Mexico. Some are permanent residents, while others are migrants that come to nest or pass through to nest elsewhere. Some are on offshore islands and waters. Around one hundred species are endemic; that is, they occur only in Mexico. The complex geography is dominated by the parallel Sierra Madre Oriental and Sierra Madre Occidental mountain chains that converge at the isthmus in southern Mexico. Interspersed are volcanoes, one of which, Orizaba, reaches over eighteen thousand feet in elevation.

Birds of Mexico, as in all parts of the world, suffer from habitat loss and other threats to their lives and activities. The American Bird Conservancy (ABC) works with a Mexican counterpart, Pronatura, to assist Mexican bird conservation. Through Pronatura, ABC supports a number of projects, for example, protection of grasslands in northern Mexico that are home to the endangered Worthen's Sparrow. Two other organizations that work to protect Mexico's birds are the Nature Conservancy and Neotropical Bird Club. All these groups merit vigorous support of any form.

I invite you to travel to Mexico through Ellie and me, to take in the natural wonders, feel the warmth of the people and of course delight in the birds. *¡Bienvenidos!*

Stauffer Miller, 2022

CHAPTER ONE

• • •

Fledglings Take Flight—1986, 1987, and 1988

First Visit

It all began on a wintry February day near the little town of Knoxville, Maryland. I was standing on a causeway of a half-frozen pond looking at waterfowl. At my side was my wife, Ellie, whom I had met through a birdwatching (now called birding) trip in 1977 and married a year later. From the house to which the causeway led came a car driven by the owner of the property, John W. Kershner, a dentist in nearby Frederick, Maryland, where we lived and worked. After making a little small talk and assuring us it was all right to look at the birds on the pond, he made a remark that, as time would show, had great repercussions for us: "If you're interested in birds and would like a warm place in which to see them, you should go to Cancún, Mexico." He said this partly because he had an interest in a Frederick travel agency, which sent clients to Cancún through the charter company Apple Tours, and partly out of sheer thoughtfulness.

Ellie at the pond where it all began.

Dr. Kershner's remark hit a responsive chord. We looked up Apple Tours, found an incredible one-week rate for Cancún, and booked a trip for Easter week, when Ellie's school was on vacation. We flew from Baltimore on a crammed Transamerica charter plane and, within three hours, replaced the cold northeast with the tropical climes of the Yucatan Peninsula. It was our first time to set foot in Mexico and first birding trip outside the United States and Canada.

When we booked our trip, Apple Tours gave us a choice of Cancún hotels, some in town and some along a strip of beach known as the hotel zone. We elected to stay in town at the Hotel America, as it was cheaper and a little more central. Once we were settled, a representative of Apple Tours met with those of us staying there. He told us to participate in activities that were part of their package, such as going to "their" beach and "their" tourist places (which undoubtedly got a cut for Apple's business). He further urged us not to rent a car or venture out on our own as there were "bandidos" and assorted other dangers. At first we abided by his advice and lounged around the swimming pool. As we did though, we couldn't help but look at the birds flying in and out of the poolside vegetation, one of which was a brightly colored one, the Orange Oriole—truly a splendid introduction to Mexico's birds.

First arrival in Mexico—April 1986.

Eager to find out what birds and sights were beyond the hotel grounds, we shrugged off the warnings and began to wander about on foot. In this first jaunt in Mexico, we came to the local bullring where I endeavored to speak to some men using what I could recall of my high school Spanish. Getting nowhere and feeling frustrated, I told Ellie that if we were to continue being off on our own in Mexico, one of us would have to learn, or relearn, the language. She said it was not going to be her.

On the second day of our visit, feeling even more adventuresome, we rented a car, a Volkswagen beetle. The car ran fine except for two small things: one, if you took your foot off the accelerator, the engine died; and two, it took both of us to turn the steering wheel. Things weren't much better at the hotel. The elevator quit working, occasioning us to move to a lower room, only to find it lacked television, refrigerator, air-conditioning, and clothes hangers.

Cancún of 1986, just sixteen years old, was a lot less developed than the mass of high-rise hotels one sees nowadays. Still existing then was decent in-town bird habitat. One such spot was a marsh across from the Sheraton Hotel in the hotel zone. A walk there just after we got our wheels brought us great looks at an incredibly beautiful bird, a Bare-throated Tiger-Heron. During this walk, we encountered another birder. He was from Toronto and knew one of Ellie's friends from that city!

On our third day, we explored the southern outskirts of the city and found a complex of roads situated in beautiful forest, the site of a future housing complex. When a man driving a steamroller there made flapping motions like a bird, we looked into a nearby tree and saw a Crane Hawk—to this day, the only one we have seen in Mexico. A day later, we threw all caution to the wind and made the long drive over to the ruins of Chichén Itzá, passing by clusters of thatched-roof stick huts with dirt floors and hammocks for sleeping, where kids, dogs, and chickens ran in and out. Contrary to what our Apple Tours representative had said, none of this looked very scary. We had a great day at the ruins, climbing the great pyramid and seeing our first of strange new birds such as euphonias and motmots. On the way back, we saw our first Yucatan Jay, the blue hues of which have to be seen to be truly appreciated. We were getting hooked on Mexico's birds.

Stauffer at Chichén Itzá, 1986.

From Cancún, you can drive in only two directions, west and south. Having gone west to Chichén Itzá, we were left with going south, which we did on our fifth day, to the small seaside ruin of Tulúm. On the way, we ventured onto a side road where we had the experience of seeing in one tree four different species of yellow orioles, all with confusingly similar patterns of black and gold. Leafing through the bird field guide to try to figure them out was great fun.

On the way back, we pulled off the road to get a better look at a perched Laughing Falcon, a black-and-white raptor that feeds largely on snakes—a fact we didn't know at the time. From a nearby hut came a family, one of whose members, Jesús, had lived in the United States and knew some English. He invited us into his hut where we took in many interesting sights, one of which was a turkey sitting on eggs in a corner. As we left, these kind people who owned virtually nothing insisted we take some ripe oranges—which were green, since ripe tropical oranges are that color rather than orange—picked from a tree behind their dwelling. We eventually planted one of the orange's seeds, from which grew a beautiful tree that adorned our house for many years.

Jesús and family near Tulúm.

Our adventuresome ways got the best of me after we got back to the hotel, and I spent the next day in bed with stomach and intestinal woes. Reasoning that I could as easily have picked up my "bug" in Cancún as out in the countryside, I reflected that if you have to get sick, why not do it having seen some distant sights. Our trip soon came to an end. Despite the balky car, room vexations and episode of illness, we had had a great time. At the airport we re-encountered our Apple Tours' travel mates. While they talked about beach and bar visits, we ran over in our minds how we had broken away from the group, seen a different side of Mexico and come out of it safely. We were ready for more.

Second Visit

In the fall of 1986, I enrolled in a Spanish class at Frederick Community College. Under the tutelage of an excellent teacher, Barbara Palmer, I easily and enjoyably relearned enough Spanish that we felt ready to do a more extended trip out of Cancún. We returned in March of 1987, again traveling during Ellie's school vacation. To our surprise, neighbors Dave and Mary Painter from Frederick were aboard our plane.

Despite the Hotel America's gremlins that turned up during our first visit, we liked its homey feel and stayed there again. To get into its parking area, a U-turn beyond a street divider had to be done. The turn was somewhat complicated, at least for us, and when we did it illegally, a policeman pulled us over. Although he insisted, in terrible English, "Ticket infraction, no jail," Ellie began to cry and implored me to act as ignorant as I could, an act I played easily. Eventually, he gave up trying to explain why he'd stopped us and let us go, probably wondering about the mental capacities of North Americans.

During this trip, my recently relearned Spanish was so bothersome to adults they switched to English rather than listen to me fracture their language. Children were more tolerant. South of town, we struck up a pleasant conversation with a boy of about ten on a bicycle, a conversation simple enough for Ellie to enter into and understand. Some of our birding we did near an elementary school. We met its headmaster, and I interpreted an exchange that set up pen pals between his school and Ellie's.

On our third day, we severed our lifeline with the Hotel America and set out on a three-day trip to the ruins of Cobá. We went south, stopping for breakfast at an old hotel in the little town of Playa del Carmen, where we sat on the verandah and Ellie ordered *pan dulce* and *plato de fruta*. We both liked the fact that just three hours away from home was this country with different birds and culture, and a language that was different yet not so much that we couldn't figure out most words. In Tulúm, we saw a hog being butchered right beside the highway. Yes, it certainly was a different culture.

We spent two nights at the Villas Archeologicas Hotel in Cobá. I had read of an unusual marsh bird, the Spotted Rail, being seen at the lake edge there, but I had no luck in finding it. During a walk in some scrubby forest near the villas, four Laughing Falcons called raucously—certainly a well-named species. However, if we had stepped on a snake, the probable source of their racket, it wouldn't have been a laughing matter for us. At a modest thatched lunch spot between the hotel and the ruins, we recognized and chatted with a Washington, DC, television personality. What an obscure spot in which to run into a celebrity! Perhaps that was the reason she was there. Our trip ended with a safe return to Cancún, and our second spring break in Mexico soon came to a close.

Third Visit

In March 1988, we made still another visit to Cancún. The plane that took us there evidently had seen long service because we learned during our flight it was from this very 727, when owned by Northwest Orient Airlines in 1971, that hijacker D. B. Cooper jumped. We again stayed at the Hotel America. Near the hotel, we discovered a near-deserted road through a swampy wooded area that ended at a clearing. The road appeared to have no better purpose than serving as a site for rubbish-dumping and who knows what other mischief. The birds, however, liked the area. It produced a Black Catbird, more common on Cozumel Island than the Mexican mainland, as well as a Bright-rumped Attila, a bird normally occurring high in the forest canopy and therefore not usually seen well. We saw it at eye level as it attended an army ant swarm, our first experience with this fascinating phenomenon of the tropics. We had to call on our field guide to identity the attila, a bird thoroughly unfamiliar to us.

Through our earlier visits to Cancún, we had seen most of the birds of its environs. We therefore drove south to the city of Chetumal on the Belize border to see if we could find some new ones. A morning's outing west of there brought us our first-ever look at a dashing little bird, a Long-billed Gnatwren. We lunched at a very basic restaurant in the little town of Ucum. After we had eaten, we asked to see the kitchen. On a small four-burner gas cooker were four large metal pots from which our lunch had been ladled—one containing milk, another pork, another chicken, and the fourth, small green tomatoes. Just before we made our visit, one of the employees, wanting the kitchen to look its best, swept its dirt floor.

After making the all-day drive back to Cancún, we decided to visit our swamp road before checking into the hotel. We parked our car in the clearing, locked it, and made about a forty-five-minute walk, never getting far from the car. On our return, we were horrified to see shards of glass scattered about the car interior. Someone had smashed a rear window of our Nissan rented from Budget and made off with traveler's checks, cash, tape recorder, and a Mexican field guide with bird records inside. After driving out to inhabited areas of town, a kind woman saw our anguish and helped us replace the traveler's checks and took us to the police station where we filled out a report. Budget was very kind. They split with us the cost of the $27 replacement window and shaved a day's rental fee off our contract, all because of our severe distress. We were keen to get back our field guide and bird notes, of utterly no value to the perpetrator but much to us. Toward that end, we went to the newspaper office and told a reporter our story. It was the most Spanish I had ever used. Although our story and a reward for information appeared in the local newspaper, we never heard a word on our stolen items.

In looking back, I suppose we were naive and careless in using the deserted road. We were also quite fortunate, as we could have been assaulted and beaten up. All in all, it was a good lesson for us. We arrived home in Maryland shaken but perhaps a little wiser.

Despojan de diversos objetos y dinero en efectivo a 2 turistas

CANCUN.- A alrededor de 300 dólares en efectivo y objetos personales, asciende el monto de lo robado a una pareja norteamericana que se encontraba vacacionando en este centro turístico. Se trata del matrimonio Miller, con domicilio en 5521 Feaqaville Lane Frederick, Maryland 21701 Estados Unidos. Ella de profesión periodista y él veterinario.

El afligido y a la vez indignado matrimonio, narró ante todo; lo feliz de su estancia los primeros cuatro días en esta ciudad, y sus entornos, a donde vinieron no sólo por la belleza del lugar, sino también por la variedad de aves que existen en este lugar, pues la señora Miller, es especialista en estos animales y ha escrito diversos artículos sobre el particular.

Sin embargo, el pasado 17 de los corrientes, a las 17 horas, se trasladaron a la avenida Bonampak a bordo de un vehículo rentado, marca Nissa, de color blanco, con placas de circulación UTB-287 Quintana Roo, para observar los pájaros que sobrevolaban el área siendo víctimas de un robo.

Explicaron, que mientras observaban las aves a cierta distancia del vehículo, a su retorno, encontraron que el mismo, -el cual habían dejado asegurado- tenía rota la ventanilla del lado izquierdo y habían sustraído sus pertenencias: una grabadora marca shack, de color negro, una nevera combinada con azul y blanca, un libro titulado pájaros de México, una bolsa de mano, color azul con café, la cual contenía tarjetas de crédito, cheques de viajero, dinero en efectivo.

Indicaron, que dichos objetos son de suma importancia para ellos, no por el valor material, sino por el aprecio moral, por lo cual dijeron estar dispuestos a otorgar una recompensa a quien proporcione datos fidedignos para la localización de los artículos. Si así ocurre, indicaron que se agrediera al Consulado norteamericano, donde tienen sus datos para localizarlos.

Castigarán a 3 agentes de Tránsito; ocultaron incidente

Por Fernando Rodríguez

CANCUN.- En tanto que el examen médico practicado en la Cruz Roja a Francisco Javier Cauich Poot luego de que éste o... un incidente de t... dictaminó que efecti... te había ingerido... embriagantes, inexplicablemente agentes de tránsito no dieron parte de los hechos y no lo registraron en la "parte de novedades" que diariamente se realiza en donde quedan asentados todos los percances que se tienen en un día.

En este sentido, el director de la corporación policiaca, teniente coronel Manuel Flores Peraza señaló

movimientos.

Luis Escribano señaló que el individuo en cuestión demostró alardes de prepo... da e incluso en la misma dirección de tránsito no demostró buen comportamiento, amenazando a los agentes que en ese momento estaban ahí y que tuvieron conocimiento del caso.

Pero, dijo, lo que es digno de comentarse, es que esta persona me amenazó de que no me volviera a cruzar por su camino porque me iba a arrepentir, por lo que

Story of our robbery as printed in *Novedades de Quintana Roo* newspaper on March 19th, 1988.

CHAPTER TWO

• ● •

Spreading Our Wings—1988 to 1995

Christmas 1988 in Oaxaca

Our scrape on the swamp road notwithstanding, Mexico was in our blood. When we read about a birding and culture Christmas trip with the WINGS bird tour company to the city and state of Oaxaca in southwest Mexico, we promptly signed up. A physicist friend Jean from the Washington, DC, area went with us. The leader of our group of ten people was Bob Behrstock, a burly fellow who sprinkled his conversation with colorful phrases. When he knew we had no hope of finding a bird we'd been looking for or were in some other difficulty, he'd remark, "We're in deep tapioca now."

Wanting us to gain some understanding of Oaxacan cuisine, he explained the complex subject of mole sauce, a regional specialty. We visited a factory producing the local type of tequila, mescal, and strolled the central plaza, or zocalo, to see elaborate scenes created with carved radishes. One evening, we joined a posada, a group of church parishioners following Joseph walking and Mary riding a white donkey. It was interesting to see another country's Christmas custom.

We did our birding in the mornings, mostly at ruins near the city and, in the course of a few days, found most of the endemic birds. On Christmas morning, we received a fine bird gift, a look at the striking and localized Ocellated Thrasher, one that had eluded us the first few days of the trip. The day after Christmas, we drove north and crossed the Continental Divide. As we looked down on fog-bathed ridges falling away to the Gulf of Mexico, Bob explained the biology of what we were viewing— cloud forests. In this region, we saw one of the world's smallest birds, the Bumblebee Hummingbird. Lower down, I was standing beside Bob when he found a bird he had never before seen in Mexico, a Slate-headed Tody-Flycatcher. At our hotel in the small town of Tuxtepec, our friend Jean and another physicist on the trip engaged in a vehement argument on some topic only physicists could fathom. At this out-of-the-way place, Ellie and I saw our first cell phones.

Our flight from Oaxaca to Mexico City took us over the crater of a huge volcano. At Mexico City airport, we saw crates of fighting cocks. As we flew toward Baltimore, an unpleasant itching crept over my body. Coming home with me was an unwanted souvenir, a severe case of chigger bites!

Palenque

Because birding tour groups frequented the Palenque ruins in the state of Chiapas, we knew of them and wanted to see them for ourselves. But getting there was not easy. With some study, we learned that the closest city with daily air service was Mérida, on the western side of the Yucatan Peninsula. We therefore decided to fly there and take a rental car to Palenque. There was, however, no way to reach Mérida from the Washington, DC, area without a stop in Miami. Our travel agent booked us seats on an Eastern Airlines flight to that place, then on to Mérida on Mexicana Airways.

As winter of 1989 moved along, labor troubles increasingly gripped Eastern Airlines. We were scheduled to fly on March 4th, the day of a threatened strike. With that in mind, we got ourselves to Washington's National Airport at 5:10 a.m., well before our 8 a.m. departure time, and were second in line when the counter opened. The gate agents didn't know if there was or was not a strike. A few pickets marched outside while, inside, the line grew for our flight 195. Television crews showed up to film our crush of hostile would-be passengers. When it became increasingly likely our flight would not depart, Eastern agents reluctantly endorsed us over to Piedmont Airlines, and we ran through the airport to get seats on its about-to-leave flight. After stops in Greensboro and Tampa, our puddle-jumper arrived at Miami in time for us to catch the flight from there to Cozumel and on to Mérida. It hadn't been easy, but we'd done it. We later found that the strike indeed occurred, and our Eastern flight never left Washington.

The colonial city of Mérida was much different from Cancún. Our hotel, the Calinda, had antique furnishings and a handsome atrium. At dinner, we chatted with two actors from New York who were in the play *Gypsy* starring Tyne Daly. With minds freed temporarily from worry about Eastern Airlines, we had a restful night, then set out on the two-day drive to Palenque. Near the ruins of Uxmal, we watched a boa constrictor cross the road. At the Sayil ruins, we birded with George and Janet Cobb, Canadians living in retirement in the Yucatan. With their help, we saw three species of tropical birds called woodcreepers. At the end of the day, we stayed at another colonial city, Campeche.

Overnight, an *el norte* weather system arrived, bringing rain, wind, and cool temperatures. In the morning, we continued toward Palenque, finding restaurants scarce and their fare spartan. Even the dogs wandering in and out of them found little. We had to settle for enchiladas, not our usual choice. Even a cup of coffee was hard to find. In the evening, we checked into the Chan-Kah cottages in Palenque.

The cold weather continued. Finding few birds at the ruins the next morning, we tried some side roads. On one, we saw quite closely a stunning Black Hawk-eagle and, on another, a Long-tailed Hermit, our first of that sort of hummingbird. Another road led to a village, where children gathered around us noisily. The boys were friendly, the girls shy. After visiting their school, we returned to the ruins, where a film crew was busy shooting a movie. Two horses escaped during filming, and the crew chased them all about. I'm not sure whether the movie was supposed to be a drama or just what, but to us, watching from atop one of the ruins, it was excellent comedy, sort of like Keystone Kops antics. Our mood became more serious during our return to the Chan-Kah when we saw a man lying dead in the highway from a road accident.

Sights seen on our drive back to Mérida included another boa constrictor on the road and a big truck that had overturned and burned. At Miami, we learned that because Eastern Airlines had declared bankruptcy, it was neither honoring their tickets nor issuing ones for other airlines. After shelling out $800, we got seats on Delta and made it home in what was a painful ending to our trip. I'm not sure whether my wish for Eastern Airlines is that they rest in peace or something a little harsher.

Colima-Jalisco

Six years went by during which time Ellie and I retired, left Maryland, and moved to Cape Cod, Massachusetts. During those years, we made a lot of trips with the Field Guides bird tour company. In September 1994, their catalog of upcoming trips arrived in our mail. In studying it closely, I realized we could do two of their February 1995 trips to the tropics with only one flight from Boston to Miami. This seemed like a good deal. Besides, February on Cape Cod was dreary. Following this plan, we did a ten-day trip to Venezuela in early February, returned to Miami, spent a night at an airport hotel—which fortunately had laundry facilities—and the next day, boarded a flight that stopped in Mexico City, then continued on to Manzanillo, a city in the small west Mexican state of Colima and near the large state of Jalisco.

In those pre-9/11 days, I habitually took a favorite scissors through security in my hand luggage. The Mexico City airport officials, however, saw them as a security threat. Not wanting to surrender my scissors, which I had bought in 1965 for a veterinary surgery class, I stood in several long lines to purchase, for six pesos, a small box that had to be reboxed, then checked. It took a lot of time, and I nearly missed the flight. To my relief, my little box came down the conveyor belt at Manzanillo, and I plucked it from amidst all the huge pieces of luggage. The scissors I still use.

The leaders of our Colima/Jalisco trip were Richard Webster and Doug McRae. Their hard work and skill got us several difficult-to-find birds. One was a thorn forest resident, the Flammulated Flycatcher. Another, on the third and last try, was a Balsas Screech Owl, under the arms of a large religious statue. One morning, before it got light, they got the beam of their spotlight on a covey of Banded Quail roosting in a shrub. We also had a good look at the hard-to-find Aztec Thrush. One day, we encountered a peasant with a burlap sack, inside of which was a huge rattlesnake that he had killed and skinned. He said he found it on a road on which we had been walking a day or so ago. Yikes! After spending almost a month out of Massachusetts, we returned to Cape Cod to find our cat well but one houseplant dead.

CHAPTER THREE

•●•

Going Cuckoo—1996 to 1997

Some birds jump right out at you when you leaf through the pages of a field guide. They have pizzazz. They're show-stoppers. When you see their picture, they make you gasp, "I've got to see this bird!" A bird eliciting this reaction from us was the Pheasant Cuckoo. Several reasons made us want to see it. One was its huge tail, about half of its fifteen-inch body length. Another was the fact that we just like the cuckoo family. Still another was that in our four visits to the Yucatan and several to South America, where it also occurred, we hadn't seen it. In the fall of 1995, we made a trip to Argentina, with John Rowlett of Field Guides our leader. Over the course of the trip, the subject of the Pheasant Cuckoo came up. John told us that one of the better spots in which to see it was in the brush behind the Mayaland Hotel at Chichén Itzá. He also made us a tape of its song. Armed with this information and technology, we made, in January 1996, our fifth trip to the Yucatan, mostly to try for the cuckoo.

We flew to Cancún, a place we hadn't seen since our robbery of 1988. Many new hotels had sprung up. We rented a car and headed west to the central Yucatan Peninsula city of Valladolid and checked into the beautiful Meson de Marques Hotel. In the trees growing in the hotel's interior courtyard, we saw several bird species, including Yellow-throated Warblers. Our room, number 123, was ideal as it put us at treetop level. We drove north, encountering a posada in one of the villages. It was the Legion of Mary, women of the town following a float bearing a statue of Mary and casting flower petals at its base as they walked. After dark, we drove ranch roads looking for the eye shine of the Yucatan Poorwill, a bird somewhat like a Whip-poor-will, but had no luck.

The next day, we drove to Cobá, where we had looked for rails some years earlier. Although we didn't find the Spotted Rail, we did find its cousin, the Ruddy Crake, one we had never seen. From there, we drove to Chichén Itzá and the relaxing Hacienda Chichén Resort Hotel, where we spent several nights. In the evening, we took a first look at the area behind the Mayaland Hotel, so as to be better oriented come morning. Not only did the hotel's security men know the cuckoo, describing its color as "cafecito" (coffee-colored), they advised us to get to the area "mañanita" (very early next morning). Although we followed this advice, we did not find the cuckoo. Making us feel even worse, when we showed the bird's picture to the hotel workers, they recognized it right away and even whistled the song.

With our three-night stay at the Hacienda Chichén used up and the time come to start for home, we downheartedly headed east toward Valladolid. As we were driving along at about forty miles per hour on a busy road about noon of a hot day, what should fly across the road in front of us but a Pheasant Cuckoo! Although we saw it well enough to know what it was, our look was far from satisfactory. Since traffic made the area dangerous for birding, there was nothing we could do except carefully note the spot and continue on our way. But now we knew a site!

Following up on this knowledge, we flew to Cancún fourteen months later in April of 1997 for a second crack at the cuckoo. We spent our first night at our old hangout, the Hotel America, now christened the Hotel Calinda America. Breakfast the next morning was a sore subject. We had unknowingly paid for it, something we wouldn't knowingly have done as we knew we would be leaving the hotel too early for it. Dismaying us even more was Playa del Carmen, where we planned to have breakfast on the old hotel verandah as we had done ten years earlier. Growth and change had come in the intervening years, transforming the formerly sleepy little place into a garish tourist trap for cruise ship passengers. Sometimes it's best not to go back.

We proceeded to the village of Felipe Carillo Puerto, where we took a room at the appropriately enough named Faisán y Venado (Pheasant and Deer) Hotel. After finding and enjoying several mixed species flocks near there the next morning, we went to Cobá, again failing to find the Spotted Rail. From there we journeyed to Valladolid and the Hotel Meson de Marques. Next morning, we went north to the coast, finding several birds restricted to Yucatan coastal scrub—Yucatan Bobwhite, Yucatan Wren and a small hummingbird, the Mexican Sheartail. We returned to Vallalodid, had a nice dinner, and retired. After many months of waiting, we were in position to try for the cuckoo at our new site.

Ellie on the beach north of Vallalodid.

April 5th, 1997, found us up early for the drive out of Valladolid to the cuckoo flyby spot. We found the area without difficulty, parked as best we could along the busy highway, and stepped out of the car. Despite the traffic noise, we could hear the cuckoo's three-note whistle. Maddeningly, however, there was no place to safely park. We drove up and down the road, searching for a way off the highway.

Finally, we saw a dirt driveway and took it. The property owner was friendly and allowed us to look around. But by then, the day had warmed so much that bird song, including that of the cuckoo, had stopped. We had one more morning to try.

Finding and seeing the Pheasant Cuckoo. (Illustration by Catherine Gausman)

Our final morning arrived. This was it. We found the dirt driveway and got off the noisy highway. We parked and began to walk, away from a house and out buildings toward a rock-crushing machine, which fortunately was idle. A Vermiculated Screech Owl called. Soon, the cuckoo began to whistle, and I taped a few cuts with my little recorder and microphone. I played back a few cuts, and the bird flew by us. I gingerly played back one more cut, and the bird flew and landed where we got a great view! The real bird was far better than the picture in the book. Our persistence had paid off. We reflected on the serendipity of it all; if the cuckoo hadn't flown in front of us in 1996, we wouldn't have seen it in 1997. I guess that's what makes birding such a great game.

Finding the cuckoo was an exhilarating moment both because it was a striking bird and because it was the consummation of a great deal of planning and physical effort. For me, it was also a watershed moment. I passed from being a casual Mexican birder to a serious one. Things took on a new light. I began to focus on how many species I had seen in the country and how many it might be possible to see. I bought a checklist of the birds and checked off all I could remember. I also bought Steve Howell's recently published Mexican field guide, the first and still only one with range maps to show distribution of the birds. Using the maps, I had the means to create a checklist of birds I could look for in a given part of the country, then use the list to score myself as to how many I saw once there. Mexican birding became a sort of test—my birding skills against my list. Several other changes occurred about this time. Ellie started a new hobby, collecting the little stickers that the banana growers place on their fruit. Since banana plantation packing sheds were an excellent source of the stickers and Mexico had lots of plantations, we had a new reason for our visits. She also began extensive use of a new technology, the internet.

CHAPTER FOUR

• ● •

Close Calls—1997 and 1999

Copper Canyon

In the 1990s, we began hearing reports of the spectacular scenery and engineering wonders to be seen by taking a train through Mexico's Copper Canyon. The idea of going there and doing the trip appealed to us. Since we were going to California for Christmas of 1997 to visit Ellie's mother, we decided to tack a little adventure on to our return trip by doing a leg of it on the Copper Canyon train, which went west to east through the Mexican states of Sinaloa and Chihuahua. Through the internet, Ellie found travel agent Raul Quezada of Chihuahua City, the capital of Chihuahua, who sold us vouchers for train tickets, meals, and hotel rooms.

Two days after Christmas, we flew from California to Phoenix, then on to the small city of Los Mochis, western terminus of the railroad. Los Mochis's airport services were meager. A single diminutive taxi was the sole means of transporting us three fellow passengers and all our luggage into town. Somehow, the driver stuffed in every person and thing. A large woman sat in the front seat between me and him. The trip of about twelve kilometers seemed to last forever. We arrived at our hotel, the Corintios, with expectation that our travel vouchers would be there. To our great shock, there was nothing, not even a message from Señor Quezada. The hotel was sympathetic to our plight. They phoned Quezada's office; eventually, his friend Hector called back with the news that the agency had gone bankrupt!

Horseman riding the rails near Los Mochis.

We were in a dilemma. We had three days in which to get across the mountains to Chihuahua City to the plane on which we would resume our trip east. Since we had planned on using the vouchers, we weren't sure we had enough money to get there. Fortunately, Ellie located a $100 traveler's check secreted in her purse. We spent a restless night and, in the morning, went to the train station early. After standing in a long line at the ticket window, we learned that first class tickets, which our agent was to have provided us, were sold out. We took what was left, second-class standing room, happy for conveyance of any sort. We boarded the train and took seats from which no one dislodged us. The train lurched forward hopefully, then stopped; two hours later, it began to inch along. If there was a schedule, it was a fluid one.

Food service on the train was colorful. Vendors hopped aboard at each little stop and came down the aisle with large open containers of coffee. For five pesos, they dipped a cup into the container and handed it to you—dripping wet from its immersion. Passengers who were train-smart got off and returned with tamales, corn on the cob, and other delicacies. Progress was maddeningly slow. Several wrecks the day before caused long delays for track repair. One especially long wait occurred when our car was in a cut, giving us nothing at which to look except a rock face. Restrooms became smelly and next to unusable. Babies began to cry. Bad as it was, it was worse in the air-conditioned first-class coaches, where toilets were as abominable as ours but windows sealed tight. We lowered the window of our second-class seat to alleviate the smell and enjoy the fresh air of a beautiful day. Open windows also allowed us to stick out our heads (with care!) to photograph and look at the engine and scenery ahead.

View from lowered windows of the Copper Canyon train.

We first passed by untidy backyards of shacks and shanties. Next came irrigated cropland, then the foothills of the Sierra Madre. Pristine mesquite and cactus forest carpeting hillocks and washes gave way to the mountains themselves, the train hugging precipitous slopes. We looked down upon wooded valleys and rushing rivers. Bridges and tunnels were frequent on this most awesome part of the trip. Fortunately, our seats were on the right, the best side to view the scenery. Unfortunately, the many delays meant we passed much of the better scenery in darkness.

We reached our day's destination, the 7,800-foot mountaintop stop of Divisadero, well behind schedule at 10:00 p.m. Let off far from the station platform onto the track bed, we struggled to pull ourselves and our luggage over the gravel, with only the stars above to illumine the way. At length, we reached stairs, which we descended to the town and our hotel. Fortunately, the hotel dining room was still open, enabling us to have a decent meal after of day of nothing but candy and cookies. We soon went to bed, totally done in.

Next morning, we took a sightseeing bus that skirted the canyon rim and stopped at lookouts. Crafts sellers with goods spread out awaited us at each stop. At noon, I toted our luggage up to the train waiting area. As I stood there, Ellie arrived with news of a bus about to leave for Creel, our next stop to the east. We took it and, in two hours, were there, a wise decision since the train came into Creel many hours later. While the lumbering town of Creel was less scenic than Divisadero, it had more hotels and tourist services.

Guests at our hotel, the Parador de la Montaña, advised us to hire a car for a morning trip to Cusarare Falls. For 100 pesos per person, we had Oscar and his van. At the trailhead to the falls, he pointed out our guide. Since all we could see was a little boy, we asked him again. Egad, this was our guide! Acting like a veteran of many such walks, five-year-old Mario, with face unwashed, nose running, clothes ragged, and dog following, skillfully led us through a forest along the banks of a small river. I was hoping for an Eared Quetzal during our walk, but did not find one. I did, however, see an American Dipper, the only one I have ever seen in Mexico. The experience of being guided by Mario and his dog was a most memorable one. We later mailed him a package of clothing.

Our intrepid guide, Mario, for the hike to the falls.

After returning to Creel, we boarded a commercial bus and completed our journey to Chihuahua City. It was a close call, but by using our wits we had surmounted our difficulties. We were never able to run down the elusive Señor Quezada. Phone calls to his home in Chihuahua City produced only his daughter, who offered a smoke screen of excuses. Follow up from home likewise led to nothing. We never got any of our ripped-off money back. We had, however, seen the Copper Canyon and, in so doing, sprinkled some spice into what would have been a ho-hum airplane flight from the West Coast to Boston.

Mazatlán—1999

In the winter of 1999, I made my first trip to Mexico without Ellie. On the cold morning of February 28th, I got up at 3:00 a.m., drove to a Cape Cod commuter bus stop and rode up to Boston's Logan Airport on a rather poorly heated coach. I flew to Phoenix on American West Airlines, receiving as the only food offered the entire flight one of my least favorites—yoghurt. At Phoenix, I met Minturn Wright, a friend from Philadelphia. We immediately proceeded to Burger King to partake of more serious food and renew our friendship. Together we flew to Mazatlán, along Mexico's west coast in the state of Sinaloa. Another friend, Cliff Pollard of Los Angeles, met us in the airport and took us out to a sedan where waited the leader, guide, driver, and fourth of our foursome, Mike Carmody of Washington State.

Our first night of this week-long outing was in a large hotel by the waters of the Pacific. Mintern, who roomed with me, didn't sleep well, and by 4:05 a.m., we were up for a 5:45 departure. At 6:00 a.m., we were in the field birding. After lunch in town, we set out on the Durango Highway, which proceeds east from Mazatlán into the mountains. Mike took us down a dirt road that looked over a canyon. Soon we heard a squawk, looked up, and viewed a flying pair of Military Macaws, one of Mexico's scarcer birds. We spent the night at the small but comfortable Villa Blanca Hotel. Next morning, he found us another scarce bird, the Tufted Jay, at about kilometer marker 206. At lunch, we chuckled about one of the local foods, gorditas, which translates as "fat little girls."

After a second night at the Villa Blanca Hotel, we checked out. I was happy to leave, as the truck noise from the nearby highway had become annoying. As we returned to Mazatlán, we searched several thorn forests for the Flammulated Flycatcher, a bird that Cliff, who had seen over seven thousand birds of the world, had never seen. For me, there was no pressure to see it; thanks to our 1995 Field Guides Colima/Jalisco trip, I had it in the bank. We were unable to find one for Cliff. From Mazatlán, we went south along the coast and stopped for lunch at a small town, where I had my favorite noon repast in Mexico—fried fish, rice, and a basket of tortillas.

Gorditas sign in Durango.

Our destination was the small city of San Blas, also along the coast. After a comfortable night there, Mike found us the striking Russet-crowned Motmot. Our car began making a terrible grating noise, possibly due to a stone under a brake pad. Mike didn't seem to want to get it repaired, fearing the rental car company would stick him with the cost. Minturn and I discussed it between ourselves, feeling it should be repaired, even if the four of us had to split the bill. Minturn suggested Mike call National Car Rental, which he did. In the afternoon, we boarded a small boat and went up a mangrove-lined channel in search of the rare Rufous-necked Wood Rail. We had an excellent look at it as it bathed, splashing water over itself. This was the eight thousandth bird seen by world-class birder, Phoebe Snetsinger.

On our final day at San Blas, we went out early to look for the Elegant Quail. We drove some pasture roads with stands of brushy cover and eventually found a covey. The key to success was the early start.

The car noise was so bad it covered the sound of a flat tire, which we drove on and shredded. After Mike changed the tire, he took the car into town where he met with people from National. Meanwhile, Mintern and I walked on a beach. With a different car, we headed north for Mazatlán. From the car, I saw a Gray Hawk I wanted to photograph, so Mike pulled off the highway. As he waited, he spotted some high-flying swifts. We all got our binoculars on them and had a good look at another special bird of Mexico, White-naped Swifts.

Fish sellers at San Blas.

On our last morning, I met three women who had just arrived from the states to do the trip we had done. Two I liked right away, Joan Weinmayr and Nancy Soulette of Massachusetts. The third, who shall be unnamed, fell into the category of dingbat. In summary, my Mazatlán outing was a great success that put me within striking distance of seeing five hundred different bird species in Mexico.

Belize-Villahermosa—1999

In mid-1999, we learned that three birds we much wanted to see—Orange-breasted Falcon, Stygian Owl and Keel-billed Motmot—could be found in the vicinity of Hidden Valley Lodge in western Belize. Since it was hardly worthwhile to travel all the way from Cape Cod to Belize for the two-day time period we wanted to devote to searching for the three, we looked for something to combine with the trip. When we learned there were banana plantations in the Mexican state of Tabasco near Villahermosa—only some two hundred miles as the crow flies from western Belize—we had that something.

Unfortunately, commercial airlines do not always fly as does the crow. Although Debby Turner of Field Guides found us flights from western Belize to Villahermosa, I was not happy with them, as they called for us to fly on November 30th from Flores, Guatemala, to Cancún to Mexico City to Villahermosa—three flights and six hours of airport-hopping to cover those two hundred miles. With this unappealing prospect looming, we left Boston November 27th and flew to Belize City. Our guide from Hidden Valley, Herman, met us and, after a long drive across his small country, delivered us to the comfortable lodge, situated in hilly pine forest. During the drive, he informed us that the owl was not at the moment using any habitual roost. Thus, our chances for that one looked slim.

The next day, Herman took us to an overlook of a large canyon into which cascaded a distant waterfall. He said to listen for the call of the falcon as it flew to a favorite perch near the falls. Despite a great deal of looking and listening, we failed to find the falcon. Eventually, rain and fog, which Herman called a norther, descended, forcing an end to outdoor activities. We spent the rest of the day in our cabin warming ourselves.

On November 29th, we left early for the ruins of Caracol, site of the motmot. The drive took about one and one half hours. Although Herman heard the motmot as we arrived, he could not locate it. More searching was unproductive, and at 11:30 a.m. we gave up, had lunch, and returned to the falls. Again failing to see the falcon, it was looking as though we were going to be rather soundly skunked. As we passed through pine forest to return to the lodge, I saw a small bird, perhaps a tanager, in the crown of a pine and told Herman to stop. I stepped out of the vehicle to look. At that very moment began a deep, repetitive hoot. Herman knew the call—the Stygian Owl—and quickly found the bird. We had a great look at what I would have thought the least likely of our three targets. Apparently, the noise of opening a car door made the owl begin to vocalize.

Jolting news hit us on our return to the lodge. Our 11:15 a.m. Flores-to-Cancún flight of the next day on Aviateca, a Guatemalan airline, had been cancelled. Although we had been placed on an 8:15 a.m. flight, this was unworkable since the Belize-Guatemala border didn't open till 8:00. The staff of the lodge put their heads together and devised a plan for us to reach Villahermosa without ever leaving *terra firma*.

Early the next morning, November 30th, Hidden Valley's personnel pressed upon us Ziploc bags of bananas and banana bread, then bid us farewell. We were now in the hands of another driver, Rennie. Over the rutted, obstacle-strewn roads of Belize we tore, at one point nearly running down a flock of Brown Jays. In three hours, we were at the Mexican border town of Chetumal, a place we hadn't seen since 1988. We moved through immigration rather briskly and entered Mexico—the first time for Ellie and me to do so in surface transport. At the bus station, we learned that two tickets to Villahermosa cost 402 pesos, of which we were short twelve. Rennie rummaged through his pockets and pulled out what we lacked. With barely time to thank him for his kindness, we boarded the bus and were off. At the stop for lunch, we could buy nothing as we had no pesos and got through the long six-hour ride on a few crackers and the food the lodge gave us.

Next morning, we rented a car at the hotel and set out for the small town of Teapa, around which lay vast banana plantations. Ellie obtained many new stickers, making our white-knuckle trip over to Villahermosa well worthwhile. Our final two days we devoted to birding. One bird I especially enjoyed was a White-crowned Parrot, since I frequently found members of that family hard to identify. With a Yellow-throated Vireo at Tapijulapa, December 3rd, my list stood at 498.

CHAPTER FIVE
· • ·

Across the Divide—2000

El Triunfo

Discerning my interest in Mexico's avian life, Phoebe Snetsinger urged me to hike the bird-rich El Triunfo Reserve, state of Chiapas. Spurred by her prodding, I signed up for a March 2000 trip there with the group that pioneered El Triunfo birding, Victor Emmanuel Nature Tours (VENT), and thus had the most experience with it. Ellie, not being an avid hiker and knowing foot travel was the only way into and out of the area, elected to sit this one out.

I had two concerns about the trip. First, was I capable enough a birder to see the many special birds of the reserve and, second, was my fifty-seven-year-old body up to a six-day trek that would take me up the Atlantic slope to a seven-thousand-foot mountain camp, across the Continental Divide and down the Pacific side to sea level? My concerns eased a little when I looked over my fellow hikers at our introductory get together at a hotel in Tuxtla Gutierrez. None appeared to be superhuman sorts. This gave me hope I could hold my own on the mountain.

The long-awaited day finally arrived. Our group of two leaders and eight participants climbed into the bed of a cattle truck that bore us down a dusty road and that, two hours later, let us out at the trailhead. Horse and mule riders (called *arrieros*) transported our heavier gear, and we began the ascent, carrying daypacks. The trail was pleasant enough but a continuous incline. I got pretty tired. After seven hours of steady uphill walking, we arrived at a mountaintop clearing. The only woman in the group, Suzanne, showed grit. Despite lagging well behind all day, she plugged away and made it. We had done it. We had gotten ourselves to El Triunfo! The place's name, "the triumph" in Spanish, now had real meaning.

With darkness rapidly approaching, we hurriedly set up our tents. Mine was a three-foot-high backpacking tent I hadn't used in years and which I loathed. I was very glad for the long night to end so I could emerge from my cocoon, stand, and move about. We had some characters among us eight participants. One, a brash New Yorker named Bob, had the temerity to question a bird identification made by our leader. Later, when our leaders announced a strategy for seeing one of the more difficult birds, Bob told me he had assisted in creating the plan—all this from someone who didn't know the birds at all well! I liked a man named Larry. He was from Morgantown, West Virginia, home of my alma mater, West Virginia University. How likely was it, we mused, that two WVU mountaineers would meet in these mountains so distant from our Appalachians?

I also liked a man named Jean, an internist from Dallas, who told a marvelous anecdote that went something like this: Around 1910, an intellectual black gentleman with impeccable British credentials was entertained at Lord and Lady Astor's home in Philadelphia. When asked which piece of chicken he preferred for dinner, he replied, "The breast please." Lady Astor rushed to his side to inform him that polite society did not countenance use of the word *breast* and that he should instead use the more socially acceptable term *white meat*. Several days later, the gentleman sent her a lovely corsage of rare orchids. With them was a note that read, "Thank you, Lady Astor, for your generous hospitality. May you wear these orchids on your white meat in remembrance of our dinner together."

After a few days at our mountaintop camp, we still had not seen one of the special birds of El Triunfo, the Horned Guan. With that in mind, our leaders sent out guides to look it and, if found, come back for the group. The plan worked. Guide Rafael found the bird, and we all had a great look. The Horned Guan is a turkey-like bird with a glossy dark body and prominent red spike, or horn, projecting from the dorsal aspect of its head. Through overhunting and land clearing, it has become endangered; the El Triunfo preserve, however, gives it some protection.

On our last day before starting down, I realized I had not seen three birds that frequented our camp area. In search of them, I set out alone down one of the trails and found all three, Mountain Robin, Rufous-browed Wren and Black-throated Jay.

After three full days at our summit camp, we began our descent to the Pacific. For the first time, I crossed the Continental Divide on foot. Though exhilarating to be there, it was also sobering, knowing my only way down to civilization was my own two legs. Boorish Bob, who was growing harder to tolerate, urinated on both sides of the divide, as if the Atlantic and Pacific Oceans would be honored to have his effluent.

Four hours of walking brought us to a crude campsite. Larry, who had a funny way of phrasing things, called it a slum. We ate freeze-dried food and drank iodine-treated stream water. When Bob stood too close to a cliff edge, Suzanne asked him to move back. "You're making me nervous," she implored. Bob's response to her concern was to tell her to shut up. Suzanne, already bruised emotionally from a bad marriage and as bad a divorce, didn't need this. I counseled the situation as best I could.

Three days of downhill plodding and two long nights along the way in my detestable backpack tent brought me to the finish line, the Pacific campsite. The place wasn't much in actual appearance, a concrete coffee-drying slab in a dusty clearing with chickens, turkeys, pigs, and dogs from a squatter's hut ambling about, the dogs snarling at us and yapping incessantly. Symbolically though, representing the end point of our walking, it was beautiful.

Civilization returned the next morning in the form of another cattle truck. A limousine could not have been more welcome. On board was a cooler of ice-cold soda and beer, our first refreshing drinks in many days. We *rode* about an hour, in triumphant mood, to the house of one of the *arrieros*, where their wives made us a fine lunch of tortillas and black beans. Another drive brought us to a paved highway at Mapastepec, where we transferred to a van for the ride to the large city of Tapachula and a hotel.

Suzanne with our *arrieros*.

El Triunfo was a satisfying experience. I had seen one of the most beautiful parts of the world; added fifty-three birds to my Mexico list; witnessed and felt human tenacity coax weary bodies up, across, and down that mountain; and enjoyed a few laughs along the way.

Nuevo Leon/Coahuila/Vera Cruz

During the El Triunfo trip, I became well acquainted with our leader, Greg Lasley of Austin, Texas. It was he who had made all the behind-the-scenes arrangements that enabled our trip to go smoothly. Through the course of various conversations, I learned he had been to northern Mexico to see Maroon-fronted Parrot and Worthen's Sparrow, endemic birds I was keen to see. Around this same time, Ellie and I heard of a banana-growing area in the state of Vera Cruz. Thus was born the plan of visiting in one trip two areas new for us.

We flew to the large city of Monterrey, capital of the state of Nuevo Leon on October 1st, 2000, rented a car, and after some difficulty, found our downtown hotel. The next day, we drove south and west into the Sierra Madre Oriental Mountains. Using Greg's driving directions, we reached rugged, pine-covered ridges and escarpments, home of the parrots. We soon heard and saw a few, an exquisite present for me on my birthday. With objective attained, we returned to Monterrey.

Home of the Maroon-fronted Parrot

Next day, we drove west to and through Saltillo, capital of the state of Coahuila, and into a ranching area called Tanque de Emergencia. Since there was no lodging in the area and we wanted to look for the sparrow at first light, we set up our two-person tent, not easily done in strong winds. Our campsite was in high grassland at the edge of a prairie dog colony. Ellie found a Ferruginous Hawk. We also saw a Prairie Falcon and a Burrowing Owl, flushed out of the ground by a coyote. The stars were brilliant in this remote setting.

Ellie at Tanque de Emergencia.

With dawn, we were soon out of the tent and, without too much work, found several of the sparrows in bunch grass tussocks upslope from our camp. On our way out, we photographed a Scaled Quail. We returned to Saltillo, got a room, and had a welcome shower. After dark, we went to the central plaza and viewed a festival of Mexican dance.

From Monterrey, we flew south to the humid Atlantic coastal city of Vera Cruz in the state of the same name and third state capital of our trip. The Hertz rental car office was the car of an agent named Racquel. She literally wrote the contract on her vehicle's hood.

We got horribly lost negotiating the large, confusing city (Raquel didn't provide much of a map), but we finally got south of it to an area of short grass prairie. Here I found my 590th bird for Mexico, a Northern Bobwhite. We continued south along the coast, turned inland, and reached our destination, the handsome colonial town of Tlacotalpan, where we got a room for $25 per night at the Hotel Posada Doña Lala. Late in the day, in what was quite a bad idea, we went for a drive around town. In crossing a speed bump (tope), one of the many thousands that beset Mexico, the underside of our car struck hard. Later, seeing the car's oil light on, I thought our car was just low on oil. To our dismay, when the attendant at a Pemex gas station added a quart, it immediately flowed through the engine block onto the pavement.

Seafood tray displayed at Hotel Posada Doña Lala.

There was nothing to do but contact Hertz in Vera Cruz, with which Doña Lala receptionist Faviola was a big help. We waited all the next day for the Hertz mechanic, who finally arrived at 9:30 p.m. and promptly repaired the torn oil pan. With wheels once again beneath us, we looked at the culprit

27

tope. It consisted of the usual mound of concrete but with one additional feature—a piece of broken steel pipe jutting from its apex. We wondered how many oil pans of low-framed cars such as our Dodge Stratus it had victimized.

Our principal reason for being at Tlacotalpan—banana sticker collecting—fizzled as our intelligence was incorrect. During our final night there, a fierce windstorm came up. As we drove up the coast the next day, we came across an incredible spectacle. The winds had driven a school of fish into an inlet. Taking advantage of this were the people of a nearby village. The men cast nets and netted the fish while waiting women processed them in what was a well-worked-out storm ritual. Above them wheeled a frenzy of gulls, terns, pelicans, and frigate birds snatching what they could. In all our travels, we had seen nothing like it. This scene, along with the broken car and getting to know Faviola, turned out to be the highlights of visiting Vera Cruz. In travel anywhere, expect the unexpected.

Sandwich Tern drawn to the fish-netting spectacle.

CHAPTER SIX

•●•

Coquettes and Quail-Doves—2001

Guerrero's Gifts

After a great deal of planning, Nancy Soulette, Joan Weinmayr, Ellie, and I set out from Boston on April 17, 2001 with destination Acapulco in the state of Guerrero. Because of Guerrero's dangerous reputation, few bird groups ventured there. Since, however, Mike Carmody (my leader at Mazatlán) had led a number of groups there without incident, we decided to entrust our safety to him in this bird-rich part of Mexico.

We flew to Dallas-Fort Worth and continued on to Acapulco, where Mike met us. We piled ourselves and our stuff into his rented Chevy Suburban and rode west along the Pacific Ocean to the small town of Atoyac. Our hotel, the best in town, had no elevator, so Ellie and I had to walk up three flights of stairs, or sixty-two steps (we counted them), to get to our room.

Our reason for coming to Atoyac was the presence in the nearby mountains of one of Mexico's scarcest birds, the Short-crested Coquette hummingbird. For our first full day of birding, we intensely scrutinized flowering Inga trees but failed to find the hummer. Surprises awaited us on our return to the hotel. We had no towels in our room meaning I descended and re-ascended the sixty-two steps so as to fetch them. As for Joan, a guest with preferred status had checked in, taken her lower-level room, and displaced her upward to a "penthouse" near ours.

Our luck turned the next day, our final chance to find the hummingbird. Despite some barking dogs, Mike found the coquette buzzing about the flowers of a requisite Inga tree. As we descended the mountain, he spotted a Lesser Ground Cuckoo flying across the road, and we hustled out of the Suburban in hopes of relocating it. As we all looked in one direction, Ellie turned and found it behind us. Some birds are no less than exquisite, and the ground-cuckoo is one of them.

We checked out of the hotel in Atoyac—with no regrets on my part—and headed for Acapulco. At the town of Coyuca, we lunched at a seafood restaurant that overlooked a colorful scene of women washing clothes in a shallow riverbed. Some scrubbed clothing at permanently set up tables while others hung it out on long lines.

From Acapulco, we headed north into the mountainous interior and spent several days birding out of the city of Chilpancingo. The morning of April 24th was a salient one. Near the community of Filo de Caballo, Mike found for us an uncommon Mexican endemic, the Dwarf Vireo. I had barely absorbed the vireo when I heard excited calls emanating from Nancy, who was downhill a little ways. Joan had urged us to be on swift watch, and Nancy had heeded her exhortation, looked up, and found several of a bird I hadn't dared hope for, one of Mexico's more sought-after species, the Great Swallow-tailed Swift. Seeing the swift and experiencing the exhilaration it produced in our group stamped into my memory an unforgettable birding moment.

Nancy spots the Great Swallow-tailed Swift. (Illustration by Catherine Gausman)

A few days later, a flyover of a Cliff Swallow at the silver city of Taxco brought my Mexico list to 599. My 600th was sure to come the next day, April 26th. What would it be? I didn't have long to think about it because early the next morning, Mike found it, a Hooded Grosbeak. I hardly had time to take in the milestone as new birds kept coming. In fact, we did a big day (an attempt to see a great many species in one day) on the 26th since we were traveling through a variety of habitats. At day's end, we had racked up 166 species, ten of which (including the grosbeak) were new to me in Mexico. I especially enjoyed a pond full of spinning Wilson's Phalaropes in the Lerma marshes near Cuernavaca.

Portions of the next two days we spent in an arduous hunt for the endemic Strickland's Woodpecker that resides in the crowns of tall pines. When we would finally get a bead on one, it would fly off, sending us scrambling in pursuit through waist-high, foot-grabbing tussock grass. More so, the weather was rainy and the light dim, all of which made staring several hundred yards into a treetop difficult. After finally getting a hard-earned look at the bird, Mike remarked that the four of us standing in a row under our umbrellas looked like a queue at a London bus stop.

From Cuernavaca, we dropped over the mountains into Vera Cruz, the state Ellie and I had visited just six months earlier. Drawing our group there were two more endemics, Sumichrast's Wren and Bearded Wood-Partridge. The wren search wasn't especially difficult, as it mostly entailed a walk into the karst hills it called home. The partridge, an endangered species hanging on in a small range in eastern Mexico, was a somewhat different story. To have any hope of seeing it, we needed a guide, and we had the best one, Pedro Mota of Coatepec. As he and his son Claudio walked, they would whistle the quavering call of the partridge. We heard it respond, but only from far off. That was the best we could do; and after four hours of walking, we called it quits, went into town, and had a late breakfast.

The Guerrero to Vera Cruz swath across Mexico yielded me forty-eight new birds for the country. While the trips Ellie and I had done on our own had been enjoyable, I had to admit that exchanging our independence for a knowledgeable person like Mike who knew where the birds were and didn't get lost had a definite upside.

Tuxtlas Tease

A goodly number of Mexico's more special birds live in small geographic pockets scattered around the country. One such bird is the Purplish-backed Quail-Dove, restricted in all of Mexico to a tiny region of southeastern Vera Cruz State. Quail-Doves walk quietly and inconspicuously along the shaded forest floor, occasionally hopping onto a tree branch. They can be very hard to see.

In late 2000, I saw an ad in a birding magazine regarding a birding trip to the quail-dove's area of Vera Cruz, a region of extinct volcanos along the Gulf Coast known as the Tuxtlas. I immediately signed up, as I wanted to see both the dove and the area. I sent a deposit to the trip's coordinator, Bob O'Dear of Observ Tours in Nashville. According to the ad, the leader in Mexico would be an expert on the wildlife of southern Vera Cruz, i.e., the Tuxtlas.

I flew from Boston to Vera Cruz on June 4th for my third visit there within the past nine months. The next morning, Bob met me. I asked about the rest of the group, and he pointed to our driver, Octavio, and said we three were it. The local wildlife expert had pulled out. Bob had not arranged for any breakfast, so from the back seat of our Chevy Suburban, I dined on potato chips and cookies. Bob had been an industrial consultant and, as such, talked at length on many interesting topics, such as utilizing flare gas from gasoline refineries.

After a day's drive, we arrived at our hotel on the shore of a lake in the city of Catemaco. Before we arrived, Bob spoke dismissively of an American ex-patriot ornithologist whom we might see hanging around the hotel, William "Willy" Shaldach Jr. Bob said he liked to bum smokes and booze, and if accompanying birders would fall asleep in their car by 11:00 a.m. Despite the disparaging comments, Bob hooked up with Willy at the end of the day, and they seemed to be fast friends as they schmoozed over beers. I didn't care for Bob's duplicity regarding Willy.

The next day, we spent the morning birding, then returned to Catemaco for lunch. Afterward, during the *sobremesa*, Bob expounded on one of his clients, R. J. Reynolds Tobacco Company, and how through that association he came up with the idea for the Winston Cup, which went on to have a long connection with NASCAR. Bob said he knew driver Dale Ernhardt, who had recently died in a stock car crash.

Guitarist in our restaurant in Catemaco.

Later that afternoon, we took a boat ride at Sontecomapan Lagoon. The boatman, called a *lanchero*, took us through a wonderful clear water channel lined by lush vegetation. I soon picked up two new birds for Mexico, Sungrebe and Pygmy Kingfisher. As we moved along, we passed a perched Collared Forest-Falcon. After turning around, we heard thrashing beneath the falcon perch, and suddenly, a medium-sized rail jumped and flew right beside our boat in good light. I saw a brown body and red legs. Bob saw a brown head. Octavio saw the brown body. We put our observations together and concluded we had seen one of Mexico's rarer species, a Uniform Crake. And we only saw it because it had been flushed by the falcon. Our boat trip through that beautiful channel, coupled with the crake sighting, rank high in my list of memorable Mexican moments.

Octavio (*left*), boatman (*center*), and Bob O'Dear (*right*) on Sontecomapan Lagoon.

The next day, we walked a trail on the slopes of the San Martín volcano. We heard some Slaty-breasted Tinamous but were not having much other bird action, so I turned back before the others. I heard one of the tinamous to my left and another to my right, seeming to answer each other, so I paused. Presently one of them walked onto the trail, stopped briefly, then walked back into cover. It was my first *seen* tinamou in Mexico, so I was pleased. Tinamous are ground-dwelling chicken-sized birds that have limited flight capacity. They are usually colored in shades of brown, making them difficult to see.

That night, we went to a savannah area to listen for a night bird, the Spot-tailed Nightjar, and we parked on a side road by a pasture. A truckload of policemen soon arrived, wanting to know what we were doing. We explained, but that didn't seem to be enough. Soon, another truckload with a superior arrived, and they copied down our driver's license information. Apparently, a murder in a nearby town had them alert for anything strange, such as a car parked on that road. Convinced at length that we were neither a threat to life and property nor in any mortal danger, they left. In wrapping up the evening, you might say the final score was policemen 11, nightjars 0.

Our best chance for the Purplish-backed Quail-Dove, as best I could determine, was at or near the summit of Cerro Bastonal. But our car wouldn't negotiate the rough rocky road that led there, and Bob was reluctant, for liability reasons, to hire an unlicensed truck driver to take us. I felt I had been badly misled since the tour promotion material advertised the dove as a possibility when, in reality, there had never been any chance for it, as I was now learning. Some honesty on that point would have been, as is usually the case, the best policy. Bob later admitted something that didn't make me feel better—that leading Mexican ornithologist Andres Sada tried to see the dove seven times before he finally did.

The last outing of the trip was to the beach of Playa Escondida, where we walked some overgrown trails. After a while, I sat on a rock in the trail. Just ahead, less than three feet from me, I heard dry leaves rustling and a fer-de-lance snake crawled into view. I had come frighteningly close to stepping or sitting on it. I quietly moved away, then high-stepped it to the car. And thus the trip ended. Despite its various teases and trials, I added seventeen new birds and brought my total for Mexico to 617.

CHAPTER SEVEN

•●•

Coast and Desert Sorties—2001

Manzanillo and Tapachula

Well offshore of Mexico's long Pacific Ocean coastline are seabirds such as shearwaters and petrels. Seeing them usually requires a boat trip. Since Ellie and I were going to Tapachula in coastal southwest Mexico to look for banana stickers, we decided to make a first stop midway down the Pacific Coast to do a seabird boat outing.

We flew to Puerto Vallarta on July 31st, rented a car, and drove to Manzanillo, the port city we had not visited since 1995. At the dock area, we negotiated with a boat captain a price of two hundred US dollars for a five-hour trip to offshore waters. Our twenty-six-foot sport fishing boat headed out early on August 2nd. To our stern, the rising sun pinked the eastern sky in a vibrant pallet.

In an hour and a half, we reached a whitened promontory rock known as *piedra blanca*. There were birds flying about the rock, but nothing too unusual, so we asked the captain to take us a little further out. That brought us good looks at Audubon's Shearwaters and Bridled Terns. By the time we saw them though, it had gotten quite hot, so we had our captain turn around, and we returned to the dock. Our trip hadn't been wildly exciting, but it had brought me a first look at two of Mexico's many offshore (pelagic) species.

Shearwaters are masters of flight in whatever wind and wave condition they encounter. With consummate skill and grace, they skim the crests and pierce the troughs, always tacking just right with their long wings. Unfortunately, they live too far from land for most people to appreciate or even know about.

Our beach hotel in Manzanillo was simple but fine for the two of us. It was elevated on posts, and as we napped that afternoon, we could hear the surf pounding with a powerful boom, all quite soporific. At dinnertime, we walked to a nearby restaurant to find a ten-man mariachi band in mid-performance. Performing with them was a comedian named Pepito, who told one-liner jokes in the style of Henny Youngman.

Some American birders had visited Manzanillo a few years before us and seen along a road to a microwave tower a skulking land bird, the Rosy Thrush-Tanager. We had seen the bird once, in Venezuela, but only by crawling into the underbrush for a less than satisfactory look at a quite beautiful bird. Hoping to improve on that, we left our beach motel early so as to drive the tower road while the morning was cool. Halfway up, Ellie heard what she thought might be the bird. I got out of the car, and just as I did, the bird shot out of dense cover to a perch where we had as good a look as can be had. It was a satisfying end to a short trip to Manzanillo.

On August 4th, we arrived at Tapachula for the second part of our trip. We rented a Nissan Tsuru, with much-needed air-conditioning, from Adolfo of AVC Car Rental. The scenery at this southernmost Mexican city was breathtaking. Dominating the skyline was the symmetrical thirteen-thousand-foot Tacaná volcano. Early morning light colored its summit in a stunning purple hue.

Tapachula has a dark side. Middle-American migrants came here in droves in the early twenty-first century to jump aboard northbound freight trains to continue their journey to the United States. Upon crossing the river from Guatemala and entering Tapachula's state of Chiapas, they encountered the most dangerous stretch of their journey, the Chiapas one. Of it they would say, "Ahora nos enfrentamos a la bestia" or "Now we face the beast." An account of Chiapas and its migrant travails can be found in *Enrique's Journey: The Story of a Boy's Dangerous Odyssey to Reunite with His Mother* by Sonia Nazario. We were not aware of any of this during our 2001 visit, and I think now that was best.

For our first night in Tapachula, we stayed at the rather expensive Loma Real Hotel. We had dinner at the hotel restaurant, and Ellie ordered the baked fish. According to the menu, it was prepared with a secret recipe. It wasn't very good, causing Ellie to remark, "They should keep the recipe a secret." The best parts of the dinner were the soup at the start and the ice cream mixed with Tia Maria at the end. After one night at the Loma Real, we moved to a small hotel beside AVC Car Rental.

On August 6th, we drove to the community of Mapastepec, a place I had seen a year earlier on the El Triunfo trip. Steve Howell's excellent *Bird-Finding Guide to Mexico* suggested a road at Mapastepec as an evening lookout for Orange-chinned Parakeet. The road was too rough for our car, so we walked up it in sweltering temperatures, found a good-enough lookout, and waited. Soon a gaggle of chattering parakeets flew by. We could see the patch of underwing yellow that is a distinctive field mark. A tasty dinner to crown our success would have been welcome, but such was not the case. The food at Mapastepec's only restaurant, the Carmelita, was wanting in several ways. If you ever happen to dine there, put any epicurean hankerings on hold. The Hotel Diana was not much better. In a heavy thunderstorm, our room's roof leaked badly at the ceiling light. We caught the dripping water in the wastebasket.

The morning air after the storm was refreshing as we drove roads through banana plantations to packing sheds, where the labels are applied to the bananas. The *jefe* at each *empacadora* gave Ellie lots of labels, many of which she had never seen. Not only were we getting life birds, we were getting life labels. As we drove through one plantation, an airplane spraying pesticide flew low over us and doused us with chemical—a hazard I suppose of banana sticker collecting.

On our last morning, we drove to the community of La Libertad, almost in Guatemala. Here we found mangroves, formerly widespread on the Chiapas coast, but now scarce. Almost immediately we found a bird we had been looking for, the White-bellied Chachalaca. In Mexico, it is restricted almost entirely to the state of Chiapas. Like its cousin the horned guan, it has become threatened from hunting and habitat loss.

When we returned our car to Adolfo at AVC, he showed his appreciation for our business by giving us a coffee table book about Chiapas. I still have it. Overall, our Manzanillo-Tapachula jaunt was a most pleasant one

Sonora and Baja

Ellie and I had been wanting for some time to see the birds and desertscapes of Sonora, the Mexican state just south of Arizona. We could have gone by ourselves but felt that we would see more birds and learn more about the desert if we went with a knowledgeable guide.

In ads, I noticed an Arizona-based bird tour company that took groups into Mexico. I contacted the company, High Lonesome Bird Tours, and explained what I wanted. The trip came together, and on December 4th, we met our guide, Wezil Walraven, at Tucson airport. With him was the fourth of our foursome, Linda Camburn, whom we had met on a bird trip in South America. Ellie and I were shown to High Lonesome's comfortable van, and the four of us went in it to Bisbee, Arizona for the night.

Linda (*right*) buying chili peppers near Baviacora.

The next morning, we crossed into Sonora at the border town of Naco, Arizona. Our tourist visas cost $20.50 per person. We drove south toward the small town of Baviacora, stopping whenever there seemed to be some birds. The best bird of the morning was an American Goldfinch, a species that winters in Mexico but does not nest. When we arrived at our hotel in Baviacora, we learned the staff was shooting woodpeckers with a BB gun because they had gotten a taste for fruit of their fruit trees. We looked at the dead "woodpeckers" and saw they were actually Cassin's Kingbirds. After an excellent dinner of corn tamales, Wezil took me after dark to a side road and whistled in a Western Screech Owl. This gave me twelve new birds for the day and brought my total for Mexico to 660.

We continued to the large city of Hermosillo and picked up a local guide, Eduardo. He took us to his parent's farm where in a pond were three new birds for me—Redhead, Canvasback and Ring-necked Ducks. A day later, we were in Bahia Kino on the Gulf of California coast. Best birds were a Golden Eagle which Wezil found and a beautiful Pacific Loon found by Ellie.

On December 8th, as we approached another Gulf of California town, Puerto Peñasco, Wezil spotted a LeConte's Thrasher flying across the road. He jammed on the brakes, got us out of the van, found the bird, and got us all to see it well. It was an impressive performance by Wezil. Ellie and I had put in a lot of time and trouble in the past in Arizona looking for this wraith of the desert, as it is often called. It was great to see one for a change without effort and stress.

Linda and Wezil bird searching near Puerto Peñasco.

Our time with Wezil and Linda ended December 10th at Puerto Peñasco when they returned to Arizona, and we boarded a bus for the second part of our trip, to Baja California Norte. At a farewell dinner the night before, Wezil revealed that he had been married to a daughter of Rankin Smith, owner of the Atlanta Falcons football team, and because of that connection, flew on the team plane and sat in the owner's box. I liked Wezil quite a lot. He was a down-to-earth guy who knew the birds well and worked hard to find them. It was also wonderful to be with Linda again.

Our bus trip to Tijuana took seven hours. The first part of it, the stretch north to Sonoyta, took us past the most beautiful Sonoran Desert vegetation I've ever seen. Further west, we moved into front seats from which we could see recklessly driving motorists passing our bus in the face of oncoming traffic.

Our Tijuana taxi.

At Tijuana, we took one of their famous taxis to the Budget Car Rental agency. In getting to our motel, we got lost and were overjoyed to get into our room finally. The next day, we drove the scenic coast road south. We immediately found Surf Scoter ducks and Black Oystercatcher shore birds. At the end of the day, we stayed at a comfortable $32 per night hotel north of Ensenada.

South of there, we enjoyed La Bufadora, a promontory where ocean waves thunderously blast air and water through a hole in the rocks. Two birds we saw nearby pleased us. The first was a Golden-crowned Sparrow, found in Mexico only in Baja California Norte in the colder months. The other was one I had looked for a few places in Mexico without success. As we looked out over some ponds, a Northern Harrier flushed a bird out of the marshes. We followed its flight with our binoculars and saw by the wing pattern that it was an American Bittern. This member of the egret family is usually quite difficult to see. We had dinner that night by the harbor in Ensenada. We both ordered Cabrilla, a fine-tasting fish of the grouper family found in the Gulf of California.

Black Oystercatchers south of Tijuana.

After two days along the coast, we headed into the mountains east of Ensenada. In pine forests, we drove over roads covered in snow. On the way back, Ellie found the bird of the day, a Lawrence's Goldfinch, at a water trough. We had seen this handsome little bird just once before.

Lawrence's Goldfinch (*center*) in highlands near Ensenada.

Back in Tijuana, Budget drove us to the US border. Ellie's cane saved us a two-hour wait in the line of people who were walking across. We took the San Diego Blue Line light rail, or trolley, to a Howard Johnson's motel and flew to Boston the next day. Our excursion into Sonora and Baja Norte had been most pleasurable.

CHAPTER EIGHT

• • •

Palenque, Cozumel, and Calakmul—2002 and 2003

Return to Palenque

Between March 16th and March 23rd of 2002, I made a return trip without Ellie to Palenque. It had not been an easy place to get to and from in 1989 and was no easier in 2002. But more on that later.

I was one of a group of four. At the airport in Villahermosa, I met our leader, Rich Hoyer of the WINGS Bird Tour Company, and participants Dutton and Caroline Foster of Minnesota. Rich struck me right away as well-organized and easy to be with. That all-important first impression was a positive one. After a first night in Villahermosa, we traveled by van to the Chan-Kah Resort Village in Palenque, the place where Ellie and I had stayed thirteen springs earlier. Birding was excellent on the grounds, and during our first afternoon there, I picked up, on my own, bird number 700 for Mexico, the colorful Crimson-collared Tanager.

Our evenings at Palenque were eventful. On one of them, we stood on a bridge over a river listening to the "pit-su" of a Spot-tailed Nightjar. When Rich tried to get the nightjar in the beam of his spotlight, his light fell instead on a Boat-billed Heron, a bird that stays in cover much of the day and comes out at dusk to feed along river banks.

Left to right: Rich Hoyer, Dutton, and Caroline Foster at Palenque ruins.

On another evening, we took a nocturnal walk along the highway in front of the Chan-Kah. As we walked, Rich played the vocalization of the Northern Potoo. Failing to get any response, we were at the point of returning to our rooms when Caroline spotted a bird in flight and asked, "What is that?" Rich got his light on it, and we had a marvelous look at the potoo. Its eyes looked huge in the beam of Rich's light. Potoos sit still as a statue during the day, often simulating a tree branch or stump then, like many of the nightjars, come out at night to forage. Their nighttime cry might be considered bloodcurdling.

I was quite taken with Caroline's Minnesota accent. After looking through the spotting scope at a bird, she would step back and say, "Beautiful, yah." Bird tours bring together people from all over our country and, with them, their many accents, all of which I find fascinating to hear.

In picking my favorite bird of the trip, I passed over gaudy tropical species in favor of an understated little brown one that nests in North America that I had never seen, a Swainson's Warbler. Rich heard it chipping as we walked a trail in the ruins, and we all had a good look, thanks to him. It is infrequently seen in Mexico because it winters in the Caribbean islands and is retiring during migration. The warbler sighting ended the trip on a high note. But then came the flight home.

Boston to Villahermosa and the reverse required three flights each way. Because both travel days were on Saturdays, they coincided with the start and end of spring break, meaning planes full of rowdy students. My last of the six flights, Atlanta to Boston, was the worst. With endurance reduced to a low point, I was crammed into a window seat with the seat in front reclined into my face. All I can say for airline travel at times is ugh!

Plover Discovery

Just two weeks after I returned to Cape Cod, we took another of our two-for-one trips—one flight Boston to Miami and two trips from there. The first part was to Jamaica, again with the WINGS tour group. The birding there was excellent, but banana sticker collecting abysmal.

On Saturday, April 13th, we flew from Kingston to Miami and on to Cancún. Several flights arriving there just before ours overwhelmed the terminal with long immigration lines and piles of unclaimed luggage. In short, it was bedlam. We finally made it through all that, boarded our Aerocaribe flight to Cozumel, and happily exchanged the chaos of one place for the calm of the other. We rented a small Volkswagen, which was adequate for the small island. Our lodging at a quiet Days Inn several blocks inland from the beachfront saved us some money and was quite adequate to our needs.

Cozumel had charm. It was nonglitzy, relaxed, and an easy place to settle into. The driving was a snap, and it was almost impossible to get lost. We resumed a practice we had not employed in a while— breakfast in the field; that is, stocking up on juice, fruit, and pastries the night before, then finding a place with a few birds for our morning repast.

Birds of the Caribbean find their way to Cozumel. One that we saw was the striking Gray Kingbird, which rarely makes it to the Mexican mainland. Thus, we were pleased to see it. A few of our North American warblers are more easily seen on Cozumel than in the rest of Mexico. Two that we encountered were Blackburnian and Prairie Warblers. The latter, found by Ellie, was bird number 740 for me in Mexico. We spent a lot of time looking unsuccessfully for the Smooth-billed Ani, an all-black long-tailed bird of the cuckoo family.

On one of our mornings, we encountered a beautiful shorebird in short grass near an air force base. After some study, we determined it was an American Golden Plover. A long-distance migrant, the bird had overwintered most likely in Argentina and was now on its way to its nesting ground in the arctic. Knowing the distance this bird had traveled and had yet to travel put us in awe. Equally amazing was the serendipitous confluence of life's forces that put it and us on this small island on the same day.

For our last night, we went to a small restaurant on one of Cozumel's back streets where tourists didn't go so much. We enjoyed talking to our waiter in Spanish. As we parted, he bade us "Vaya con Dios." His warm-hearted wish stayed with us the rest of the evening, the next day as we traveled home, and for many days after.

Ants Perchance?

After reading in several magazines about the ruins of Calakmul, Ellie and I decided to do a January 2003 trip there, even though hotel information was sketchy. As with our 1989 Palenque trip, we flew to Mérida and rented a car, this time a Ford from Avis. We felt relieved to see we were indeed in Mérida since our Cape Cod travel agent never learned to call the place anything except Madeira.

We made a counterclockwise loop through the western Yucatan with first stop Celestún, situated along the Gulf of Mexico and famous for its American Flamingos. We stayed at the Hotel Maria del Carmen. It was a strange stay in that no one ever collected any money from us for the room. In the evening, a local bird guide, David Bacab, visited us. He said the flamingos could often be seen from a nearby bridge.

The next morning, I awoke early, and while dressing, my eyeglasses came apart. After splinting them with a toothpick and duct tape, I went to the bridge and saw a line of about forty flamingos, just where David had suggested. They are resplendent birds in any light but especially in that of early morning. After returning to the motel and getting Ellie, we again failed to rouse any hotel staff so we put some money in an envelope and slid it under the office door. We'll never know if we underpaid, overpaid, or were pursued by the police.

Our next stop was the city of Campeche. Here I learned a new Spanish word, *optica*, the place that repairs glasses. We found it and got them repaired, no charge. We walked Campeche's gulf-side promenade and savored its tangy Yucatecan lime soup.

South of Campeche, a semi had jackknifed, blocking both lanes of the highway. The only way around was by taking one's car over a steeply pitched shoulder that was overgrown with brush. Cars began trying this route and managed to do it, albeit putting car and driver at a severe tilt. My turn came, and I warily took our Ford across the incline. Avis never found out.

Wrecked semi and first car moving past the impasse.

At the turnoff to Calakmul, we discovered there was indeed a hotel, but quite a basic one, cabins of sticks and thatch in a wooded setting. Although primitive, it beat camping, for which we had prepared. As we lay on our beds that afternoon, we heard leaves rustling outside and lifted our heads to see an Ocellated Turkey, bird number 746 for me. A Vermiculated Screech Owl called after dark.

Our "hotel" of sticks and thatch at Calakmul.

The next day, provisioned with food, water, and a full tank of gas, we set out for the ruins. The sixty-kilometer (forty-mile) entrance road was paved but narrow due to encroaching weeds and brush. We arrived at a small headquarters building and paid our thirty pesos per person fee to enter. Our climb to the top of the tallest pyramid rewarded us with a panorama of undisturbed forest expanse falling off to all sides. That view, one we had only seen in magazine photos, we now relished in person.

As we returned to our car, we heard the chirring of some ant tanagers. "Might there be an army ant swarm?" we asked ourselves. We sat on our camp stools and waited. As we did, we recalled the splendid ant swarm we experienced near Cancún in 1988. Birds are attracted to an ant swarm because it stirs up insects that are easy pickings for them. Some birds live almost entirely off insects flushed by ants and, because of it, are called obligate ant followers. For birders, an ant swarm is exciting because of the surprise element; there's no way of knowing what birds might be drawn to it.

Presently, three woodcreeper species—Barred, Ivory-billed and Tawny-winged—arrived at the ant swarm. Just feet from us, they watched the ground intently for scurrying insects. A few wood wrens and a Yellow-breasted Chat soon joined the action. The final bird to arrive, however, was the star of the show, a bird we had never seen and one almost always with ant swarms, the Ruddy Woodcreeper. It has a rust-colored body, bluish facial skin, and an odd tuft or pouch of feathering on the throat. The woodcreeper grand slam was the highlight of our trip.

After leaving Calakmul, we headed north for Mérida, stopping en route in the town of Ticul, where we stayed at a hotel facing the central plaza, or zocalo. We had dinner in the hotel restaurant, and Ellie enjoyed the *pollo pibil*, a Yucatecan chicken dish. Our waiter, named Sidney, was quite friendly. We told him that in our week in the Yucatan, we had not found a restaurant that had flan, an everyday Mexican dessert. He said his restaurant, like the others, had none, but he offered to run down the street a block to the corner grocery, buy some, and bring it to our table. And that's how we got some flan.

Our flight from Mérida to Miami went well, but on the 7:25 p.m. one to Boston, we heard a loud noise as our plane pushed off from the terminal, after which the plane abruptly stopped. The tow bar had broken, so the ground crew had to get another. When we were finally airborne, the copilot gave updates on Boston's temperature. First it was eighteen degrees, then thirteen, and then eight! After the tropics, it was a shock to stand outside the terminal at 11:30 p.m. shivering in the taxi line. We finally got to my Nissan Sentra parked at a friend's house, and to my amazement, it started. We walked into our Cape Cod house at 1:30 a.m.

CHAPTER NINE

Rivers, Ruins, and Runaway Cows—2003

Usumacinta River Trip

In addition to the Calakmul ruins, I had been wanting to visit those of Bonampak and Yaxchilán in far southeast Chiapas State. Since bird tour groups didn't go there, I looked for a group that did. In my research, I came across Ceiba Adventures, which advertised a boat trip down the Usumacinta River, starting in Guatemala and ending at Yaxchilán. Although the emphasis of the trip was archeology, I knew that where there were ruins, there would be birds. Since the trip promised to be rigorous, Ellie elected to tend the home fires.

On March 8th, I flew from Houston to Villahermosa on Continental Express and met the group at nearby Palenque. Our leader was Joe Orr of San Antonio. He was tall, outgoing, and had three main interests—rivers, astronomy, and Mayan culture. Participants besides me were Stanford University professor Janet and Southern Mississippi professors Stella and Jean.

Our motorized boat on the Usumacinta River.

We went to the little Palenque air strip and squeezed ourselves and our luggage into a six-seat single-engine plane. My tiny rear seat and compartment so constricted me that my knees pressed against my chin. Surrounding luggage pinned me in place. The pilot was apprehensive that we were overweight, but he gunned the engine and down the strip we went, just clearing some treetops as we made our ascent. Once airborne, he felt he could handle the plane so he took us on a southeasterly course, and an hour later, we arrived at Flores, Guatemala.

Over the next two days, we traveled by motorized river boats to visit Guatemalan ruins. At one visit, I stayed on board and chatted with one of our boatmen, Porfirio. He asked me a lot of questions about how he could get himself a United States girlfriend—as if I would know anything about such a matter.

On the third day, we transferred to a larger boat at Sayaxche, Guatemala, and took on firewood, grates, propane cylinders, and all importantly, crates of beer. Our crew also changed, to principal boatman Don Julian, his son, two other boatmen, and two Guatemalan policemen. Things were beginning to feel like an expedition.

Our galley on the Usumacinta River island.

We left Sayaxche at midmorning and headed down the Rio Pasión. I eagerly awaited its confluence with the Rio Salinas, because at that point, we would be on the Usumacinta, with Mexico (and its birds) off the port side. We reached the confluence at 3:15 p.m., and a half-hour later, Joe shouted, "Scarlet Macaws." I scrambled forward to watch a pair of them fly above us, then slant off into Guatemala. Janet, in her capacity of professor of mechanical engineering, applied principles of physics and mathematics to certify I saw the macaws in Mexico. These splendid birds have been nearly extirpated from Mexico due to habitat loss and the caged bird trade. I felt quite fortunate to have seen them.

Our mess on the river island.

Around 5:30 p.m., Don Julian steered our boat to a landing on a sandy river island, and camp was soon set up. The crew prepared an excellent dinner for us, and after dark, Joe gave us an astronomy lesson, pointing out some of the planets in the star-studded sky. That night, as I lay in my tent listening to the waters of the Usumacinta lap against our beach, I thought of many things. Foremost were my thoughts about the place I was in—island, river, surrounding forest. Because no road had ever reached any of it, it was truly wild. How difficult, I thought, has it become to find such places. Soon enough, I would be back in civilization, but for this one night, I felt far from it.

The next day, we broke camp early and were soon under way. Our boat passed by a wooded canyon over which soared a White Hawk, King Vulture, and several raptors I could not identify. Around 11:00 a.m., we arrived at the Mexican settlement of Frontera Corozal. This was as far as Don Julian and crew were to take us. They had treated us well, and parting was a little sad.

A few hours later, we journeyed down the Usumacinta, now in the hands of Mexican boatmen, and disembarked at Yaxchilán, an impressive riverside ruins. I separated from the group for a while. When I rejoined it Joe—a much better birder than he let on—said he had heard manakin wing-snapping noises near stele 11, so I went there. At first I heard nothing, but soon heard the noise. With a short walk into the forest, I found several fine-looking White-collared Manakin males. The male's wing structure is specially modified to produce the odd snapping sound, which attracts females. After a visit to Bonampak, we rode by van to Palenque to complete our air-water-ground circuit. The trip had been enjoyable. The group had accepted me, the non-archeology interloper, most heartily. Jean kindly invited Ellie and me to come to see some historic sites near her home in Mississippi, but we never followed through on the invitation.

Oaxaca Circuit

Around one hundred or so of Mexico's birds are found only within its borders. These endemic species are understandably highly sought after by birders, Ellie and I included. Since Michael Carmody's May-June circuit trip of Oaxaca-Chiapas-Oaxaca offered a fair chance of success with several endemics we had not seen, we signed on. A friend from Cape Cod who had never visited Mexico, Sally Leighton, joined us.

Sally, Ellie, and I flew to Oaxaca City on May 21st. During our taxi ride to our hotel, we watched the rather chaotic scene of several horsemen with lassos chasing a runaway cow in and out of traffic. Welcome to Mexico, Sally. Before meeting our group, we took a day to show her some local sights. At a restaurant near where men were making tequila and mescal, the waiter's first greeting to us was "Which to you want?" We declined both. We tried to show Sally the zocalo that Ellie and I remembered fondly from our 1988 visit with Bob Behrstock, but striking teachers staging a sit-in protest blocked the streets and thwarted us.

Oxcart in Oaxaca.

Others in our group were Dan and Ann from Florida and a young man named Ebba. Since Ebba had a foreign accent, we asked him what country he was from, and he quickly replied, "California." He was actually from Sweden. Leader Mike and we six participants began our birding in the mountains north of Oaxaca City where, on May 23rd, I saw an Azure-hooded Jay; with that sighting I had seen all of Mexico's seventeen jay species. Seven are endemic, and most are quite striking.

We next looked for birds on the Pacific side of the Isthmus of Tehuantepec. Mike took us on a side road into a thorn forest, and we came across a small seep that was attracting some birds. With careful watching, we found two endemic species, Sumichrast's Sparrow and Rosita's Bunting. Swiss ornithologist Francis Sumichrast collected specimens of these birds in this area in the nineteenth century. He also collected a wife, Rosita ("little rose" in Spanish). He did something for her that few husbands can do—he named a bird for her, but not just any bird, the beautiful Rosita's Bunting. It is said that he considered Rosita to be as beautiful as the bird, and vice versa.

Indian family at San Christobal de Las Casas.

Bonito catch on dock at Puerto Angel.

From low elevation at the isthmus, we traveled to high elevation (7,200 feet) at San Christobal de Las Casas. Early one morning, when still dark, we walked a trail in a pine-oak forest where Mike hoped to find a Bearded Screech Owl. Just as day broke, we heard the owl's soft trill. We soon found it and had a terrific look. Nocturnal owl searching is often unrewarding, but when success occurs, as in this instance, the satisfaction is enormous.

For the last stop of the trip, we visited the fishing village of Puerto Angel tucked among Pacific Coast headlands. Our reason for being there was to do a pelagic trip. The deep waters not far offshore promised a few ocean species. From a concrete dock, we gingerly stepped into a pitching twenty-seven-foot boat. Just as Mike was boarding, the boat lurched and so threw him off balance that he dislocated his shoulder. In a lot of pain, he left in a taxi with Dan and a local man for a small hospital, where he was put under anesthesia and the shoulder bones put back into place. The rest of us disembarked and hung about the dock, watching fishermen unload their catches of bonito, a type of tuna. As for the pelagic trip, it never happened.

On the final day of our tour, as we drove north from Puerto Angel toward Oaxaca City, we noticed a profusion of insects in the highway. Furthermore, local people were picking them up and holding them by the wings in order to bite off and eat the abdomen. The insect, a large ant known as a chicatana, is a Oaxacan delicacy. None of us were inclined to try one.

The aborted boat trip was a topic of much conversation among us. We tended to agree that some higher power signaled to us through the medium of Mike's accident that the trip would be unsafe and we'd be better off remaining on shore. Regarding the rest of the trip, though, it was rewarding in that Ellie and I saw six endemic birds, three owl species, a dozen different hummingbirds, and several interesting raptors, just to name a few. Once again, it proved wise to go with a guide like Mike, who knew the birds and where to find them. As I flew home, my Mexico bird list stood at 790. The countdown to 800 was on!

CHAPTER TEN

Chihuahua and Sonora Reprises—2003 and 2006

The Pine Cone Parrot

When Rich Hoyer, my guide at Palenque in 2002, invited me to go with him for a July 2003 outing to look for two special birds of Chihuahua State's Sierra Madre Occidental Mountains—Thick-billed Parrot and Eared Quetzal—I jumped at the opportunity. A friend from Cape Cod, Dick Jurkowski, joined me. Again, the trip was too rigorous for Ellie.

Dick and I flew to El Paso, Texas, where we met Rich. He picked up a rental Jeep Liberty, and we crossed into Chihuahua at Ciudad Juarez. Thirty kilometers south of there, we had an immigration stop to obtain stickers, stamps, and documents required of rental cars going into interior Mexico. The stop took nearly three hours.

After finally resuming our drive, Rich pointed out a nighthawk that had a flight pattern different from Lesser Nighthawk, which I had seen in Mexico. Rather, the pattern was that of Common Nighthawk, thus number 791.

We reached Chihuahua City late in the day and spent the night in a Hampton Inn. The next day, July 1st, we stocked up with groceries at a Super Walmart, then headed west toward the mountains. At a bridge over the Rio Santa Isabel, a long-tailed bird sallied out over the river and landed in a willow. It was a Yellow-billed Cuckoo, number 792.

We left the paved road at the village of Matachi and began a long, torturous stretch of cobbled road that was in many stretches as rough as driving in a stream bed. From my rear seat, I watched Dick's head and body thrown about in his front seat as we bounced along. He must have been thinking something like "What has Stauffer gotten me into?" but if he had such thoughts, they went unsaid. In fact, he seemed to be enjoying chatting with Rich and taking in the beautiful pine forest into which we were ascending.

Three hours into our jouncing ride, Rich heard some bird chatter. We jumped out of the Jeep and had a fine look at Thick-billed Parrots. They were a hat trick for me—life bird, Mexican endemic, and bird number 793. A short time later, Rich found number 794, a Townsend's Solitaire, a thrush species I had seen often in Utah when Ellie and I lived there in 1978.

Thick-billed Parrots formerly lived in Arizona, but they are now extinct there. They are the only extant parrot species that formerly resided in North America. They range widely in Mexico's Sierra Madre Occidental Mountains in search of pine cones, which they shred to get at the pine nuts.

The parrot numbers are decreasing in Mexico, possibly because they rely on old Imperial Woodpecker holes for nesting, and the woodpecker has become extinct. The woodpecker, the world's largest, is a story unto itself. Author George Plimpton and several accomplished birders searched fruitlessly for it in the 1970s in the area we were now in; even then, it was thought extinct. Plimpton wrote about his party's search and, to a lesser extent, the parrot in an excellent article published in the November-December 1977 issue of *Aububon* magazine. The article, entitled "Un Gran Pedazo de Carne," can be read online.

Night had fully set in when we reached our destination. With a great deal of fumbling around in the dark, we set up our sleeping arrangements. After that, we met our local guides, Diana and Javier, who served us a delicious dinner topped off with cans of Dos Equis, chilled to perfection in our cooler. And after that, it was bedtime.

At dawn the next day, July 2nd, we heard Thick-billed Parrots as we lay in our sleeping bags. Few are the places on earth where the sleeper awakes to that sound. With daylight, we could survey our surroundings. Our lodging, quite the contrast with the previous night's Hampton Inn, was the loft of a forty-by-forty-foot log hut. To ascend to it, we climbed a rickety wooden ladder with no handrails, then stepped over two large logs. That brought us into a room with sloping roofs and low eaves, akin to a haymow. The hut was in a broad clearing bounded by coniferous forest that spread upslope on three sides. Our elevation was around 8,000 feet.

Thick-billed Parrot feeding on pine cone. (Rich Hoyer photo)

Dick Jurkowski at our bunkhouse.

After breakfast, taken on the tailgate of the jeep, we went in two vehicles, Javier leading and we following, in search of the quetzal. He separated from us but kept in touch, and in a few hours, he came running and whistling that he had found it. We excitedly walked a ways and then had a great look at another hat trick bird for me (number 795).

On our way back to our bunkhouse, as I called it, Javier stopped our caravan and walked into a ravine in search of a nesting hawk. The hawk he didn't find, but he did find something better, a Saw-whet Owl. He came for us, and we saw the owl well. While we watched it, Rich heard the notes of another owl, investigated, and found a Northern Pygmy Owl. In quick succession, I had recorded numbers 796 and 797. Seeing two difficult-to-find owls in one location within five minutes left my head spinning.

July 3rd was our last full day at the mountain camp. In the afternoon, we did something all three of us needed to do—bathe. One by one, we entered a small room beneath our quarters and, by use of dishpans and washtubs, got the job done. That night, we walked in rain in search of a Flammulated Owl, which Rich thought might be in these mountains. With persistence and a lot of time waiting under umbrellas, he found the owl and got his light on it to enable us a good look. This small owl was not only Mexico bird number 798 for me but also a life bird.

We made our departure July 4th. It took all morning to get down to the paved road and a gas station. I was relieved to get there since the jeep's fuel warning light had come on. At the end of the day, we reached the small town of Nuevo Casas Grandes and its small motel. Our stay there brought the comfort of sleeping in a bed, something our bodies craved after three nights on an air mattress on a hard floor. I suppose there are many ways to celebrate our nation's birthday. We did it by stretching out in a bed.

We spent our final morning, July 5th, birding in washes and mesquite scrub sixty miles south of the New Mexico boot heel. Early that morning, an obliging Crissal Thrasher popped into view atop a shrub, and we saw it, number 799. What would be number 800?

After the thrasher sighting, Rich parked in a wash studded with aspens and willows. Lots of birds were moving about, but breakfast, a final tailgate one, came first. With cups and saucers washed and put away, we were ready for birding.

Protruding upward from one of the willows were bare sticks. We watched them closely as they were perfect hummingbird perches. Soon a male hummer landed. I could see the long slightly decurved bill and black gorget. It was a Black-chinned Hummingbird, number 800 for me! Congratulations and high fives came from Rich and Dick. It was great to reach the 800 milestone, but it was even better to do it in the company of good friends. I scarcely had time to absorb the moment when Rich found number 801 for me, a Cassin's Sparrow. This was scary. Was I now in pursuit of 900?

"Tire"less Sonora Birding

In late 2005, Ellie and I moved from Cape Cod to Charlottesville, Virginia, and in early 2006, friends from the Cape invited us to join them on a bird tour they had arranged to Mexico's Sonora State. Although the tour would cover some territory we had visited with Wezil Walraven five years earlier, we accepted the invitation.

On March 20th, we met our group in Tucson. With them was our leader, David MacKay of Wezil's High Lonesome tour company, who lived in the town of Alamos in Sonora. Not just our leader, he was also driver, cook, bird finder, and jack-of-all-trades. Just as in 2001, we crossed into Sonora at Naco, Arizona. An hour or so south of there, we stopped at a dried-up stream that had a few residual pools of water. As we looked around for birds, my friend Ned Handy pointed out a duck and asked me to look at it. To my surprise, it was a Hooded Merganser, one of Mexico's scarcer birds.

Later in the trip, we ascended the west slope of the Sierra Madre Occidental to the village of Yecora, where we birded along a stream that attracted birds despite being litter-filled. Amidst the debris was an old tire and, beside it, a Wilson's Snipe, found by me. Later we birded along another littered stream, but this one had few birds. "The reason is obvious," pointed out another friend Tom Prince. "No old tires." Humor continued to enliven the trip. While birding near Ciudad Obregón, Steve of our group christened the place Lake Wobegon and said he had spotted Garrison Keillor.

Near Ciudad Obregón, we came across a remarkable sight. A large truck had upset and spilled cases of eggs onto the roadway. Cleaning up the mess was a front-end loader. We commented that spread over that highway was the biggest platter of *huevos revueltos* you'd ever see.

One day, we drove to the Gulf of California coast. While looking out over the water, Steve spotted a brown bird flying in line with the horizon and thought it might be an immature gull. Dave looked at it and identified it as a Parasitic Jaeger. It was my first ever sighting of a jaeger in Mexico and bird number 809 for me. Jaegers chase gulls and terns in order to steal their food. They are the pirates of the bird world.

As our tour ended and we headed north to Tucson, we had lunch at a picnic area beside a din-filled highway at an Hermosillo toll booth. Dave noticed some bird activity across the highway and went to investigate. I went with him. The first bird to come into view was a Bendire's Thrasher. With more looking, we found two little birds with gyrating tails. They were Gray Vireos, birds that winter only in Mexico and then in a small range. This was a personal milestone. Twenty-six vireo species occur in Mexico, and with this one, I had seen them all. Mexico's vireos occur from one tip of the country to the other and occupy all sorts of habitat niches. Seeing the thrasher and vireos at the tollbooth showed that birds can be in the most unlikely of spots, even along a busy highway. A few hours after the picnic stop, we crossed the border at Nogales and concluded another satisfying sortie into Sonora.

CHAPTER ELEVEN

• • •

Gulls and Galloping Coyotes—2007 and 2008

Search for the Masked Duck

I am enamored with all birds but especially those that live in marshes. This is because one family of marsh birds, the rails, is among my favorites. Also I simply enjoy a marsh's ambience.

Flooded pasture in the Villahermosa marshes.

The largest marsh in Mexico and one of the largest in the world is the lowland northeast of the city of Villahermosa of Tabasco State where two rivers slow their course and spread out as they empty into the Gulf of Mexico. Within this vast wetland are many bird species. One of them is the Masked Duck. Most ducks are not so difficult to see, but this one is an exception because it hides in waters overgrown with marsh grasses.

In my many trips to Mexico, I had not seen this secretive duck. With that in mind, I contacted Rich Hoyer, who had been my guide twice in Mexico, and asked if he might be available for two days in March to do birding in the marsh with emphasis on the duck. He was amenable to the idea. Two friends from Boston, Herman D'Entremont and Eva Casey, were also interested. So we had a foursome.

Left to right: Herman, Eva, and Rich at Villahermosa marsh.

Yellow-crowned Night Herons at the marsh.

The trip went like this: In early March, Ellie and I flew to Orlando, Florida, where we visited relatives. After that, we drove to Fort Myers, Florida, planning to see a Boston Red Sox spring training game. But that plan fizzled because the game was sold out, including standing room beyond the outfield. We couldn't even get tickets from scalpers. Thwarted in our initial plan, we fell back on other activities and had a very good time. There is indeed life beyond baseball. A few days later, Ellie flew home and I flew to Houston where I met Herman and Eva. The three of us then met Rich at the Villahermosa airport.

Vermillion Flycatcher at the marsh. (Rich Hoyer photo)

In our two days of birding in the marsh, we failed to find the Masked Duck, but we did see an extravaganza of other birds—egrets, herons, ibises, bitterns, shorebirds, too many to name. All of us got wonderful photographs. Mine of a Green Heron and line-up of Yellow-Crowned Night Herons are favorites. Rich got a knockout photo of a Vermillion Flycatcher. In the little settlement of Jonuta, we had a delicious fish lunch in a riverside thatch-roofed restaurant on stilts. Sometimes what stands as a first objective, be it a baseball game or the Masked Duck, turns out to have its equivalent or even an improvement in its replacement.

Green Heron at the marsh.

Cruise on the *Zaandam*

The birder who has seen eight hundred of Mexico's bird species and wishes to see some of its remaining two hundred or so runs into challenges. That is because the remaining ones tend to be (1) secretive, such as owls, rails, or the Masked Duck; (2) scarce; (3) only present in certain seasons; (4) inaccessible, such as on off-shore islands; and (5) oceanic. The question becomes how much time, effort, and money the birder wishes to invest to see, and often fail to see, some of these birds.

While pondering that question in mid-2007, I learned that the Charlottesville Senior Center's travel office was offering an eight-day San Diego-Acapulco-San Diego cruise on Holland America Line's *Zaandam*. The trip had appeal for two reasons. First, it was a means of getting into deep Pacific waters to see Mexican pelagic species, and second, it was sufficiently nonrigorous that Ellie could join me. My act of signing us up for the cruise had a double significance. In the short term, it meant we were going on the cruise. And long term, I was committing to continuing with Mexican birding and trying for some of those two hundred species. Or as the saying goes, I was in for a penny, in for a pound.

The *Zaandam* departed San Diego on October 26th and, over the next two full days, traveled over eight hundred nautical miles. From the promenade deck, I was able to identify Red-necked Phalaropes, Black Storm Petrels and Pomarine Jaegers. On October 28th, I got a photo of an immature Sabine's Gull resting on the water. The Sabine's Gull nests on tundra in the high arctic and then migrates south well at sea to winter in the Pacific off South America. It was a thrill to see it, and only by being aboard a ship in these waters at this time of year was it made possible

Immature Sabine's Gull.

We came to anchor October 30th in Acapulco harbor, and I took an excursion on a fishing boat. Although there were slicks full of birds, I couldn't get the boatman to move in close enough for me to see them well. The highlight of the outing was a large pod of dolphins. Two fellow passengers from the *Zaandam* annoyed me greatly, exclaiming when these beautiful creatures leaped and splashed, "Oh it's a whole s———load of them." Why must people profane the wonders of the natural world with their vulgarity?

On the return to San Diego, the *Zaandam* called at Cabo San Lucas. Ellie and I disembarked at 8:00 a. m. and hired a taxi to take us fifteen kilometers north to a small resort where we had read that the endemic Xantus's Hummingbird occurred. We paid the owner ten US dollars to search his grounds for the hummingbird but failed to find it.

From there, we began walking a dusty road that led past some scrubby growth that looked promising for birds. Ellie's whistle brought in not only the hummingbird but also another endemic, the Gray Thrasher. With our bird mission accomplished and the day getting hot, we were thinking about how we might get back to the *Zaandam* when a white sedan came along and stopped. Out of it stepped a young Mexican man who spoke excellent English. He had a proposal for us. If we would listen to a ninety-minute sales promotion about some condominiums, he would give us US$150, T-shirts, lunch, and a ride to the ship. I was hesitant, but Ellie liked the deal. So we got in the car and off it sped, taking us still further from the ship.

At the condos, the sales pressure was intense. We were handed off from one sales person to the next, each a little more hard sell. On and on it went as minute after minute went by. They even tried the world's oldest sales tactic, sex, sending out a buxom young woman with plenty of cleavage. Finally, Ellie grew weary and began proclaiming, "You're making me very nervous!" And she didn't say it just once or in *sotto voce*. That seemed to break them, and ever so reluctantly they handed over the money and T-shirts and called a taxi for us. We boarded the *Zaandam* just minutes before her sailing time, both of us breathing sighs of relief.

Although we enjoyed the cruise and I saw a number of new birds, the most memorable part of the trip was the condominium episode. We told that story many times to family and friends. Our daughter was appalled that her mother was so beguiled by the promise of $150 that she would step into a stranger's car in a strange place. And no, we did not buy a condominium.

Chihuahua Grasslands

During the Masked Duck trip of March 2007, I spoke to Rich Hoyer about a winter visit to the grasslands in northwest Chihuahua State. I had read about the area and its wintering birds in an article in the *American Birds* Christmas Count issue of 2002–2003. Rich knew the area and was agreeable to going there with me.

The first leg of the trip, as with several previous Mexico ventures, was the flight from the East Coast to Tucson. My seatmate on the January 9th flight was a Baptist minister's wife. We conversed widely, and the topic of evolution presently came up. A born-again Christian, she had never met someone such as I who believed in it. She kept saying humans couldn't have just evolved; if so, how would they get a soul? I am not sure I held my own with her, but I did my best. In any case, it was an engaging way to pass time on a flight. You never know who you'll meet in the great airline seatmate lottery.

I met Rich at the Tucson airport, and we picked up a rental Saturn SUV that had a feature I first heard of with that car, Sirius XM radio. After passing the night at Douglas, Arizona, we crossed into Mexico on January 10th at Agua Prieta and headed east on Highway 2. Soon after entering the high savanna of the Animas Valley, we spotted a raptor perched on a post and identified it as a Rough-legged Hawk, a bird that nests in tundra areas of Canada. The few that get into Mexico do so only in winter and usually go no further south than the region we were in. The hawk was a thrill to see, partly because of the unexpectedness of it and partly because it is such a fine-looking bird.

While we were stopped to look at the hawk, Rich's keen ears picked up the flight call of a small ground bird, the Chestnut-collared Longspur, again a bird only in Mexico in the winter. We followed the longspur in its bounding flight, found it when it put down, and had a good look. Another winter visitor, a Cooper's Hawk, perched on a nearby post.

Cooper's Hawk in Chihuahuan grasslands.

We continued east on Highway 2, and near the settlement of Janos, we watched a White-tailed Kite eating a cotton rat. At dusk, a Short-eared Owl flew in front of our car. Rich stopped the car, stepped out, and made a squeaking noise that brought the owl back for another pass.

Just minutes later, we witnessed an exciting grasslands chase. A coyote in pursuit of a jackrabbit was so intent on catching dinner that he or she sped along, oblivious to us in our moving car. For long distances, car and coyote ran parallel within feet of each other. We could hear and see the coyote huffing and puffing. Occasionally, he or she would glance over at us, eyes glowing in the dimming light, all the while not breaking speed, stride, or focus. Overtaking darkness prevented us from knowing the winner of this contest of speed, stamina, and wits.

The *American Birds* article listed Sprague's Pipit as a bird that could be seen in the grasslands. Ellie and I had seen this songbird in the 1970s in North Dakota, but only as a dot in the sky as it performed its aerial courtship song. I had never seen the bird well. In hopes of remedying that situation, Rich selected an expanse of short grass where the pipit most likely would be, and through it, we walked. It wasn't long before we spotted the bird and had an excellent look as it strode in front of us. The dark eye stood out and reminded me of another bird of short grass, the Upland Sandpiper. Although finding the pipit was great, even better was just being out of the car and walking in beautiful terrain. That in itself was a splendid, unforgettable experience.

Scrub Jay in a Chihuahua woodland.

One last highlight came our way. Some of Rich's Arizona birding friends had visited the grasslands a week earlier and reported some Long-eared Owls. We went to the site and walked a ditch lined by hackberries and willows. Suddenly, we began flushing the owls, five of them. They flew along the ditch and landed where we could see them well. They are truly beautiful birds, but since they are masters of concealment, few people have seen them. With this sighting, I registered my nineteenth of Mexico's twenty-nine owl species.

On our return to Tucson, we tried for Juniper Titmouse but without success. But no matter! I had seen enough birds to send me home with fine memories. And I had also seen the interesting habitat where many birds that nest in North America pass the winter.

CHAPTER TWELVE

· ● ·

Migrants and Marsh Birds—2008 and 2009

La Pesca

Four years after Ellie and I were married in 1978, we birded the Galveston-to-Brownsville portion of the Texas Gulf coast to take in the spectacle of migrant birds coming north with the spring. It was a wonderful seven days in April.

Remembering that 1982 trip, I wondered if I might experience some of that same migration except along the Mexican Gulf coast. But where along it? The answer came when I saw a report by Bob Behrstock, our leader in Oaxaca in 1988. He reported an April bird survey he had made of a ranch near La Pesca, a fishing village at the mouth of the Rio Soto La Marina, state of Tamaulipas. Since he had seen lots of spring migrants there and La Pesca lay just 150 miles south of Brownsville, I felt that a trip there could be both productive and easily done. All I needed was a guide.

I noticed an ad by Tropical Birding Tours company that listed trips they conducted in Texas and Mexico. I contacted the company, told them what I wanted, and soon engaged Tropical guide Michael Retter to take me to La Pesca. We agreed that four days would be the right number for our tour.

I met Michael on April 27th, 2008, at the airport in Harlingen, the closest city to the border that had an Advantage Car Rental office. Michael liked Advantage because it had, in his experience, an impeccable record of providing clients the correct paperwork for Mexico. Alas, that record did not remain so. We did not have the right papers when we went through the checkpoint on the Mexico side, forcing us to recross into Texas (after a long wait in a long line of cars) and return to Advantage. Armed with the correct forms, we returned to the border only to find we had to take another crossing well to the west.

Finally free of the border and its large congested city of Matamoros, we had a pleasant drive south. Near the turnoff to La Pesca, we came across a highlight of the trip, a ribbon of perhaps twenty Mississippi Kites flying above us. These raptors feed aloft on large insects. At La Pesca, they were nearing the end of their long spring migration from southern South America to nesting sites in the southern Great Plains. Over eons generations of them have made this journey. Long may it continue!

After we got settled in our simple but adequate hotel rooms, we went for a drive and discovered a dirt road that bordered brush and heaps of trash. In essence, it was the town dump. But birds were abundant there, and we soon found Scarlet Tanager, Dickcissel, and Blackpoll Warbler, all in migration and new to me for Mexico.

Scarlet Tanager along the La Pesca dirt road.

The next day, we rose early and headed for some foothills covered in thorn forest. We heard parrots and soon had a good look at a pair of Yellow-headed Parrots, now scarce in Mexico because of trapping for the caged bird trade.

Fishing boat at La Pesca.

At dinnertime, we had a craving for red snapper. This seemed like a reasonable wish since the fishing boats had it as part of their catch and almost every business facade read "Se Vende Pescado" (fish is sold). Oddly though, no restaurants had snapper. At our last stop, a woman brought out a tray of five freshly caught robalo (snook). Each of us pointed to the individual fish we wanted, and she prepared our choices perfectly. We were, however, a bit slack jawed to see a whole sliced uncooked garlic clove atop each fish. I suppose it was *pescado* La Pesca style.

On our return to the border, Michael wanted to visit salt marshes at the Mexican side of the Rio Grande delta to look for a bird that barely reaches Mexico, the Seaside Sparrow. But deeming the area unsafe, he decided against going. Across the border in Texas, he took me out to the US side of the delta. The river's mouth is surprisingly narrow, thus its name of Boca Chica, meaning in Spanish "small mouth." And thus ended a short but highly productive and interesting excursion to experience the Mexican aspect of the spring Gulf migration.

Tecolutla 2009

Although I much enjoy marsh birds, especially that elusive group that lives therein, the rails, I had seen few of those birds over the years in Mexico. Thus, when I read in Steve Howell's excellent bird-finding guide to Mexico that rails could be found at Tecolutla, a coastal village in northern Vera Cruz State, I was interested. Once again I contacted Rich Hoyer about being my guide, and once again he was agreeable.

Moo softly or carry a big stick.

I had to make three flights to get to Tecolutla. The last was on Aeromar Airlines. We six passengers for the flight were driven across the tarmac at Mexico City airport in a van. From it, we watched our plane fueled. Once aboard, we promptly took off, and an hour later, we arrived at Poza Rica, the closest airport to Tecolutla. I was glad to see Rich as the day had been tiring.

Our first day of birding, April 18th, was a busy one. At first light, Rich took me to a bird-filled marsh. Although we saw several Sora rails, we did not see two rarer ones I was hoping for, King Rail and Yellow-breasted Crake. Birds were not the only wildlife at the marsh. A large alligator kept an eye on us. Cattle milled about, including one hobbled by a large forked stick attached to prevent it from breaking through fences.

Later in the morning, we drove ranch roads, and I became the official opener and closer of gates. Crested Caracaras stalked the pastures in search of prey. We came across and watched a colorful scene of a family cutting up and boiling pork skin so as to make the popular snack chicharron. It is usually deep-fried, but this family chose boiling. We did not sample it.

Crested Caracara in Tecolutla pasture.

We had lunch on the beach and, in the afternoon, walked a causeway through a marsh in search of an endemic bird, the Altamira Yellowthroat warbler. After much work, we got a good look at one. It is a truly beautiful bird. As an appetizer at dinner, we had *pulpa*, or shredded manta ray. We felt the pulpa could be improved with a little onion and mayonnaise.

Altamira Yellowthroat. (Illustration by Catherine Gausman)

The next day, we made a long walk into a pasture where grew stands of knee-high grass. From one stand, we flushed a Barn Owl. Another held a singing Sedge Wren. The day grew hot, and I got very tired from the walk. A cold drink at our lunch spot was most welcome. Rich had *tostados de camarones* (shrimp), and I had mojarra, a type of perch. Grilled to perfection and served whole, it was delicious. In the afternoon, Rich found an Upland Sandpiper in a pasture. I don't know how he found it as it was at great distance and nearly obscured in heat haze. Much closer was a flock of migrating Long-billed Dowitchers in beautiful breeding plumage.

Rich's platter of *tostados de camarones*.

Flock of Long-billed Dowitchers.

A day later, we separated, he returning to Arizona and I flying to Virginia. We did not find the targeted rails. But I knew that finding and seeing such birds was always a long shot. The Altamira Yellowthroat stood out as the highlight bird of the trip. Since there are few places in the world where it can be seen, I felt privileged that I had gotten to one of them—and been there with someone who could help me see it.

CHAPTER THIRTEEN

● ● ●

Rocks to Rain Forests—2010 and 2011

One (or More) Good Terns

Some birds are only in the Yucatan Peninsula in the summer. And since I had never been there in that season, I stood to gain a few birds by going then. I contacted Rich Hoyer again, and we arranged a June trip. A young birder, Tim of Nelson County, Virginia, went with us. I was surprised that the plane from Atlanta to Cancún was full of Americans. I couldn't fathom why my countrymen and women would travel to a warm place like Cancún when the weather was warm at home.

On June 18th, 2010, we checked into a plush hotel in the hotel zone. The grounds were large enough to contain a college campus. Like the plane, the hotel was brimming with Americans. We had a reason for lodging at this hotel, the Dreams Cancún Resort and Spa. Offshore were rocks where we had hopes of seeing some unusual terns. And the only place that afforded a view of the rocks was this hotel.

From a shaded lookout behind the hotel, we went on tern watch. Tim promptly proved his worth by finding a flock of Sooty Terns flying over the rocks. Upon resuming our watch the next morning, Rich found another fine-looking tern, a Brown Noddy, perched on a buoy near the rocks. Sooty Terns and Brown Noddies spend most of the year well out to sea. If they are to be seen from shore, it would usually be in the summer months, such as June, when they are nesting just offshore on rocks or sandy reefs.

From Cancún, we traveled south and made a stop at a botanical garden to search for a bird that had long eluded me in Mexico, the White-necked Puffbird. We did not find the puffbird. Rather, something found me—deerflies. Their bites made my knuckles swollen and sore. At day's end, we took rooms at the village of Bacalar in a simple motel that was quite the contrast to the Dreams Cancún Resort and Spa. That evening, we had a dinner of fajitas while listening to a television panel of Mexican soccer analysts discuss the upcoming World Cup competition. During commercial breaks, Tim told entertaining stories.

Rich had received a report of a large stork, a Jabiru, near the Mayan ruins of Tzibanche, southern Yucatan; so on our third day, we searched for it. After failing to find it, we entered the ruins. When Rich heard what he thought was the vocalization of a puffbird, we looked up and saw that the sound was coming from a soaring Great Black Hawk. And soaring with it was a bird I had wanted to see, a Plumbeous Kite. The kite winters in South America and only makes it to Mexico in the summer months. It was a principal reason for being in the Yucatan in June. The kite put on a great show above us, swooping and diving, perhaps in pursuit of large insects such as dragonflies.

Cattle on road near Bacalar.

Tim and Rich at Tzibanche ruin.

Plumbeous Kite at Tzibanche.

Rich and young helper birding at Cobá.

After the morning at the ruins, we began our return to Cancún. At Felipe Carrillo Puerto, we checked into a small hotel and, at dusk, went to the forested Vigia Chico Road for night birding. The heat, humidity, and mosquitos were abominable. As compensation though, we heard and saw birds. Best was a Yucatan Poorwill. It makes a song like a Whip-Poor-Will's but more rollicking. We also saw two owl species. As we walked along the pale limestone road bathed in moonlight, I saw a small snake slither into view. I hollered at Tim and Rich, who were ahead of me. They turned around, and Rich shone a light on it, revealing it was the poisonous fer-de-lance. It was agitated. When Tim bent over for a photograph, it struck at him.

Our next to last stop was at another Mayan ruins, Cobá, a place I last visited in 1996 with Ellie. My luck there with the Spotted Rail was no better than in 1996. Leaving off the rail search, the three of us walked around, taking in the beauty of Cobá. I could see why the Mayans would have chosen it to construct a temple and monuments. Ringing its large lake were several small villages and the ruins. As night drew on, lights in the villages began to twinkle. At the same time, the setting sun pinked the lower horizon while sending beams of light streaming skyward. It was a magical way to end the day and our summer outing to the Yucatan.

Sunset over the lake at Cobá, June 21st, 2010.

Lacandón Rain Forest and Maya Ruins

Forming part of Mexico's southern border is an arrowhead-shaped protuberance of Chiapas State that juts into Guatemala. Within this salient lies the Lacandón rain forest, the most northern such forest of the western hemisphere. Some of the many birds in this rain forest range no further north. The Lacandón Mayans have long made their home here.

In the fall of 2010, I learned that my guide and travel companion, Rich Hoyer, was leading a trip to the Lacandón through his bird tour company, WINGS. Although I had seen some of the region and its birds on my 2003 Usumacinta River trip, I reasoned that by going with Rich I would see birds I had not seen then.

I met Rich and the rest of our group at February 12th, 2011, at Villahermosa. We four participants were Bob and Eve from Oregon, Bill from California, and me. The first day consisted of a long drive from Villahermosa to Las Guacamayas Lodge along the Lacandón River. That evening as we stood beside the river, I heard a piercing "yee-oww" sound from the opposite bank. I thought it might be an owl, but Rich said it was a Great Potoo, the larger cousin of the Common Potoo, which Caroline Dutton had found on my Palenque trip of 2002. Although we could not see the whole potoo, we could see its large eyes shining through the darkness. It was my 870th bird for Mexico.

The next day, we went on a morning boat trip on the Tzendales River. Lined by pristine Lacandón wilderness, the scenery was breathtakingly beautiful. Our boatman knew the birds, and he pointed out a spot where he had seen the elusive White-necked Puffbird. A little whistled imitation of its song brought in the bird for all to see. Finally! Yippee for me!

In the afternoon, we visited a grassy roadside ditch that was home to a family of Gray-breasted Crakes. These small rails made lots of calls from the grass, but not one could we lay eyes on. According to the books, these birds should not be in Mexico. But creating accurate range maps for secretive birds such as the crakes and rails is a challenge for ornithologists.

On our last morning at Las Guacamayas Lodge, February 15th, we walked the main road and found a Rufous Mourner perched on a tree branch. This member of the flycatcher group makes a harsh shrill call sometimes likened to a wolf whistle. After that, we hiked a hilly trail through the forest. Although I got tired, I was glad I kept up with the group because Rich spotted a handsome Black-throated Shrike-Tanager. Settled in at mid-level in the forest, it would have been easy to overlook despite its bright colors. Around this time, I received a painful bite or sting on the outside aspect of my right ankle.

Rufous Mourner. (Rich Hoyer photo)

Black-throated Shrike-Tanager. (Rich Hoyer photo)

Just after we left the lodge, we came across six King Vultures feeding on a dead cow. We watched them from our vehicle. Since they are usually seen as soaring specks, this close look was amazing. Vultures don't get a lot of love—no one wants to be called an old buzzard—but they are vital to the world's ecosystems.

King Vulture at the dead cow site.

Our second stop of the trip was at Frontera Corozal, gateway village to the two ruins I had visited in 2003, Bonampak and Yaxchilán. As soon as we entered the grounds at Bonampak, Rich found a splendid hummingbird, the Purple-crowned Fairy. Mexico has over fifty species of hummingbird. They are found in every sort of habitat and, in the case of the Fairy, lowland rain forest. Later, he showed me a little bird high in the canopy that is rarely seen in Mexico and thus had Rich excited, a White-vented Euphonia. One last bird wrapped up a productive morning at Bonampak, a Ruddy-tailed Flycatcher. It was bird number 880 for me in Mexico.

Group climbing the Acropolis at Yaxchilán. (Rich Hoyer photo)

Yaxchilán produced an exciting hummingbird, a Black-crested Coquette. It hovered just long enough at some mid-story flowers for us to see the important field mark, a pale rump band. We made a steep uphill hike to an acropolis at Yaxchilán. It was grueling, at least for me. I'm not sure what the others thought. We all had a long rest before starting down. A day later, the trip ended, and our group, which had been a compatible one, parted.

After returning home, the ankle that had received the bite or sting on February 15th became red and sore. Not only that, the lesion robbed my foot of needed strength to press the accelerator pedal of my car. I began visiting my dermatology office where a nurse practitioner, Chelsi Miller, took an interest in my case. After several visits, she thought she could see puncture marks in the sore area and took a photo. As the days went by, I could increasingly feel something moving beneath the skin. Chelsi told me to buy some bacon and apply it to the lesion, which I did. After lifting off the bacon a day later, I could see larval processes extending out through the puncture marks. I now had a diagnosis.

Sunday, March 13th was a big day. Chelsi met me at the dermatology office, which she opened just for me. She anaesthetized the area, opened it surgically, and removed two botfly larvae. Each was about a centimeter in length. My speculation is that a fly or wasp, carrying the botfly eggs in its mouthparts, stung my ankle on that forest trail in Mexico and deposited eggs, which matured into larvae. I was fortunate the larvae were in my ankle. I can think of far worse bodily locations to have a burrowing botfly!

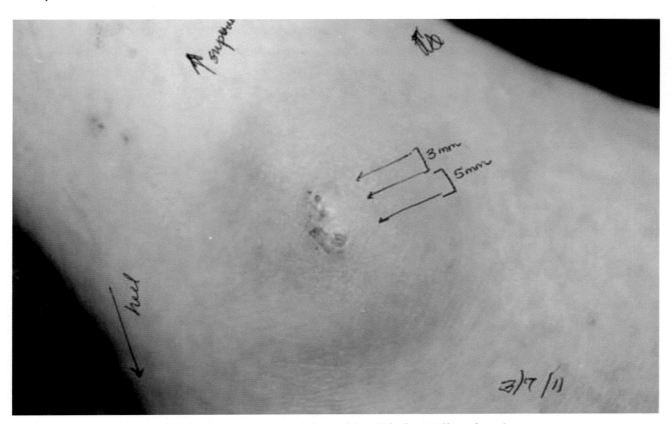

Botfly lesion on my right ankle. (Chelsi Miller photo)

CHAPTER FOURTEEN

• ● •

Last Adiós—2013

While my ankle slowly recovered, Rich and I discussed doing a pelagic trip. He felt that August at the southern tip of Baja California Sur would be the optimal time and place. With that decided, I flew to San Jose del Cabo on August 18th. Our motel was comfortable and had the amenities of a pool and nearby ocean, neither of which I tried.

I studied the bird list before leaving home and saw that a bird I had not seen, the Whip-poor-will's cousin the Common Poorwill, might be possible. I alerted Rich about this, and he came prepared to make a search for it. After dinner, under a full moon, we went to some nearby hills. Swarms of gnats plagued us. After much listening (and swatting), we heard our target bird calling at great distance. Over the next half hour, it came much closer. The poorwill sings out its name "poor-will!" with emphasis on the second syllable. Hearing that perky song that night was a great experience.

The next morning, we went to a marshy area in town and found a bird not just endemic to Mexico but also to Baja California Sur, the Belding's Yellowthroat. This little warbler is threatened due to destruction of its reed bed habitat. In the afternoon, we joined forces with one of Rich's friends, a birder named Steve, and his friend, Gerardo. We went to a lookout to watch for seabirds flying past, but saw few.

Boarding our Zodiac. The dog stayed behind.

Our waiting fishing boat.

The next day at the town of Los Barriles, our foursome boarded a Zodiac that took us from a beach out to a waiting twenty-nine-foot fishing boat. We passed over a few pods of dolphins and saw several species of shearwaters and storm-petrels. The most interesting pelagic bird was a young Red-footed Booby that was hitching a ride on the back of a sea turtle. Boobies are large seabirds with long, heavy bills. Like a dagger from the skies, they plunge into the sea to seize their food. We also saw an elegant bird of tropical oceans, the Red-billed Tropicbird, which was a thrill for Gerardo, who had never seen one. A casualty of the boat trip was my nose, which sustained a severe sunburn.

Booby on board.

On our last day, Rich and I visited some irrigated fields near the city of La Paz. A small pond in one field was filled with shore birds. As I flew home, I looked over my list and saw that the last new bird species for me for the trip, the Red-footed Booby, had nudged me to 889 birds seen in Mexico. Would the booby be my last?

Shorebird flock in pond near La Paz.

AFTERWORD

Life and circumstances closed in on me after my Baja California Sur trip of August 2013. Chronic illness that increasingly gripped Ellie required my care. Furthermore, I was developing my own infirmities. Last, I could not justify travel to far-off Mexico to see at best one or two new birds for that country. The Baja trip and the Red-footed Booby were indeed my final *adiós*, my final wings across the border.

As I think over the twenty-seven years in which Ellie and I (or I and others) traveled to Mexico, certain moments stand out. My mind runs to that morning in March 1986 when we first stepped away from the Hotel America in Cancún and made a walk about town, a walk that opened our eyes to what we considered to be the real Mexico. That short outing, which we did only at Ellie's urging, was auspicious because it was a springboard to future adventures in Mexico.

Also, I think of the August 2001 morning in Tapachula, Chiapas State. Upon rising early, we stepped outside our hotel to be stunned by the purple hues coloring the slopes of the volcano Tacaná. As ephemeral as they were beautiful, the hues soon disappeared. Only in aurora's light had they been visible. Again, I think it was an openness or a readiness to see what the world had to offer that put us in the right time and place to experience that volcano.

A pearl of wisdom that has long guided me is by Thoreau: "Only that day dawns to which we are awake." I am grateful for all the joys Mexico and its birds have given me, and that I was granted dawns there to which I had the good sense and fortune to be awake.

APPENDIX

· ● ·

List of Guides Used by Ellie and Stauffer in Mexico

Guide	Company	Year
1. Bob Behrstock	WINGS Tours	1988
2. Doug McRae/Richard Webster	Field Guides Tours	1995
3. Mike Carmody	Legacy Tours	1999
4. Greg Lasley Victor	Emmanuel Tours	2000
5. Mike Carmody	Legacy Tours	2001
6. Bob O'Dear	Observ Tours	2001
7. Wezil Walraven	High Lonesome Bird Tours	2001
8. Rich Hoyer	WINGS Tours	2002
9. Joe Orr	Ceiba Adventures	2003
10. Mike Carmody	Legacy Tours	2003
11. Rich Hoyer	WINGS Tours	2003
12. David MacKay	High Lonesome Bird Tours	2006
13. Rich Hoyer	WINGS Tours	2007
14. Rich Hoyer	WINGS Tours	2008
15. Michael Retter	Tropical Birding Tours	2008
16. Rich Hoyer	WINGS Tours	2009
17. Rich Hoyer	WINGS Tours	2010
18. Rich Hoyer	WINGS Tours	2011
19. Rich Hoyer	WINGS Tours	2013

INDEX

Printed in the United States
by Baker & Taylor Publisher Services